The
GIRL GUARDS
OF WYOMING
The Lost Women's Militia

Dan J. Lyon

Foreword by Jim Allison, Supervisor of Collection, Wyoming State Museum

THE
History
PRESS

Published by The History Press
Charleston, SC
www.historypress.com

First published 2019

Manufactured in the United States

ISBN 9781467140751

Library of Congress Control Number: 2019937049

Therefore, whether you eat or drink, or whatever you do, do all to the glory of God.
1 Corinthians 10:31

In memory of my mom, Connie, for her love and encouragement (miss you!);
to my brothers, Mike and Dave, for your support; and to my sister, Kim,
for running my errands.

Contents

Foreword

My family has close ties to Wyoming history. My grandmother had a wonderful old album of faded, often grainy family photographs depicting grandparents, aunts and uncles and long-forgotten cousins who lived out their lives in the state. During my grade school years, I spent hours at her house examining those ghostly images in detail, getting to know my ancestors' faces. Grandma sometimes went through the album with me, relating stories she could remember. Her father had been a Wyoming state senator in the 1890s, her grandfather a territorial councilman in the 1880s. But as much as she could tell me about the men in the family, she had little to say about the women. She may have thought I wouldn't find their accomplishments exciting enough, and because of my age at the time, perhaps she was right. Today, I greatly regret not asking for more stories of my female ancestors. My grandmother did, however, make one cryptic statement about a woman in a photo that stayed with me for decades. Pointing to an image of the Cheyenne Bicycle Club from the late 1800s, I asked her why it was in the album. She indicated a shy-looking young woman in the group and murmured something about it being her aunt who "had something to do with the day Wyoming became a state." It would be years before I would discover what role that young woman had played in Wyoming's statehood celebration.

My interest in history eventually led to a job at the Wyoming State Museum. Quite a few years ago, while examining firearms in the collections, I came across what appeared to be a wooden toy rifle.

Curious, I pulled the records to discover it had been used by a member of what was termed Wyoming Girl Guards Company H in 1890 during the celebrations surrounding Wyoming's entry into the Union. The rifle had belonged to a young woman named Mabel Tupper, but what really caught my eye was the photo of Company H in the files. As I looked over the names that corresponded to small, handwritten numbers next to each member of the company, the name Lavina Grainger jumped out at me. Close examination of the photo and a little research revealed that Lavina Grainger was the same shy woman in the Cheyenne Bicycle Club photo—my great-great-aunt.

Since that day of discovery, I have been fascinated with the history of Wyoming's Girl Guards and have serendipitously found numerous others with the same interest. But until now, the Girl Guards' many stories have never been told in one narrative. I'm extremely grateful for this work because without it, my aunt's story, and those of many others, would have remained a largely forgotten footnote to Wyoming's past. Dan Lyon's book noting the young women who composed Companies H and K, along with the historical context of how the Wyoming Girl Guards came to exist, is long overdue.

—JIM ALLISON,
Supervisor of Collection, Wyoming State Museum

Acknowledgements

Special thanks to Suzi Taylor, reference archivist (extraordinaire) at the Wyoming State Archives, for helping me solve a more than 125-year-old mystery surrounding Wyoming's forgotten women's militia. She patiently researched and scanned photographs and, at one time, literally shed some blood when she cut her finger pulling nails from an original solid wood backing (you could see the tree rings!) from a class of 1892 photograph because a spiderweb of dried masking tape obscured the image. And thank you to Jim Allison, Wyoming State Museum collection supervisor. I've known Jim since high school and recently discovered he is related to an original member of the Girl Guard. How cool is that? I am grateful for Jim sharing his family history in the foreword.

This manuscript is a culmination of more than eighteen months of research that included sifting through more than 1,600 firsthand documents and hundreds of photographs. That daunting task was made possible in large part by the Wyoming State Library, the Wyoming Newspaper Project, the Wyoming Genealogical Society, the Colorado Historic Newspaper Collection, the Library of Congress, Google Books and the National Archives. Photographs are courtesy of the Wyoming State Archives (WSA) unless otherwise noted. Artist renditions are by the author.

Introduction

The legend of Wyoming's forgotten women's militia hearkens to Wyoming statehood and the women's equality movement. The territory was founded in July 1867 and was branded a maverick in 1869 when John A. Campbell, Wyoming's first territorial governor, signed a bill granting women the right to vote. When Wyoming petitioned for statehood in 1889, the issue of women's suffrage was a hot button topic divided by two parties of public opinion. Many prominent Cheyenne citizens favored suffrage and statehood, but one dissenter was a prominent Cheyenne judge whose daughter was a member of Company K. The judge threatened to "move to Alaska if Wyoming became a state."

The first legislative assembly on December 10, 1869, endorsed the women's suffrage movement and included women's right to vote in the Wyoming constitution:

> *Section 1.—Every woman of the age of twenty-one years residing in this territory, may, at any election to be holden under the laws thereof, cast her vote. And her right of the election franchise and to hold office shall be the same under the election laws of the Territory as those of electors.*

The section in the state constitution on this subject read:

> *(Section 1, Article VI.)*
> *The rights of citizens of the State of Wyoming to vote and hold office shall not be denied or abridged on account of sex. Both male and female*

citizens of this State shall enjoy equally all civil, political and religious rights and privileges.

Section 27 of the state constitution said: "Elections shall be open, free and equal, and no power, civil or military, shall at any time interfere to prevent an untrammeled exercise of the right of suffrage."

Shortly after Wyoming women were granted the right to vote, Wyoming appointed Esther Hobart Morris as the first woman justice of the peace in February 1870. She was followed by the first all-woman jury, the first woman to serve as a bailiff (Martha Symons Boies Atkinson) and the first woman in the nation to vote in a general election (Louisa Ann Swain).

The constitution, however, exempted women from military service. Article 17, section 1 said, "The militia of the State shall consist of male citizens of the State, between the ages of eighteen and forty-five years." Contrary to this, Company K paved new ground as the first and only fully trained women's militia in the nation. Company K earned major ink from coast to coast as its performances were reported throughout Wyoming and in major newspapers in Washington, D.C.; Pittsburgh; Denver; Omaha; Santa Fe, New Mexico; Astoria, Oregon; and Sacramento, California. A Wyoming newspaper editorial suggested sending the military maidens to Washington to "show our statesmen what the girls can do in the militia…and admit that the women of Wyoming at least were deserving of statehood."

Some 125 years later, the legacy of the Girl Guard has become a footnote found in a manila file at the Wyoming State Archives in Cheyenne. I became interested in the Wyoming Girl Guard militia while working at the F.E. Warren Air Force Base museum. One day, while I was looking at a photograph of the Seventeenth Infantry marching on the parade field at Fort D.A. Russell, my boss, Paula Taylor, asked me if I could see the Girl Guards in the background. I could, but they were barely visible. The Wyoming Girl Guard militia earned its ink when Wyoming marched to statehood, but post-statehood coverage of the event was minimal, even at the twenty-fifth and fiftieth anniversaries of statehood. The Wyoming Historical Society featured a sidebar on Company H in the 1965 edition of the *Annals of Wyoming*, but a complete history has never been written.

I have a confession: I never intended to write a book about the Wyoming Girl Guard Militia. When I began researching its history to satisfy my curiosity, I saw two sepia-toned photographs that started me on this journey. This manuscript is dedicated to the memory of the unsung heroines of the Wyoming Girl Guard Militia.

"The Girl Guards"
Have you seen our "Girl Guards," known as Company K?
With their miniature muskets and caps of gray!
Have you heard the tramp of their delicate feet
Keeping perfect step to a cadence sweet?

Enchantingly sweeping in fitful air
The kaleidoscope march of these maidens fair;
Who forth from a land of Elysian bloom
To pass in review only seem to have come.
O, what can compare with their beauty and worth
But the Deity's smile on the bosom of earth!
Just heard, did you say? Then I'll tell you more,
Concerning each one of this bright twenty-four.

Stand here close by me where the footlights burn,
Where Company K makes many a turn;
To the right or to left, as the case may be,
Not as they respond to the reveille
Will you see them, but each in her proper place
In line, when they move with such charming grace,
And as they appear by the tactical grade
In the practice drill or a grand parade.

Gallant Colonel Stitzer is in command,
You have heard of him oft—stay, the girls are at hand;
First Emma O'Brien and Kate Kelly too,
Brighter, nobler girls Cheyenne never knew;
Mary Davidson, handsome—in girlhood a queen,
The intellect flash in her eye to be seen;
With fair Gertrude Morgan make up the full set.
Yet no; I mean the first Girl Guard quartette.

Next come Lulu Maxwell and Alvenie Gloye,
And then Gertrude Ellis and sweet Mamie Horrie,
As charming a four you will scarce ever see
These are second in line in K Company;
Handsome Eva Smalley with wealth of dark hair,
With Iona Davis, both winsome and fair,

And then Edna Wilseck and Carrie Ingram,
Two bright, charming misses, in unison come.

Three fours now have passed us—just one-half in all—
As they now countermarch through the well lighted hall.
Look! look you again! as the column sweeps on!
Here come Ada Johnston and Clara Newman,
Two as pretty young misses as ever you'll see,
While the fair Isabel Montgomery
And sweet Bessie Vreeland, excelling in song,
With steps of perfection, come marching along.

Then Jessie Lee, a bright, fair-haired lass,
Ora Cowhick, a beauty, quick near us pass;
Then Mina McGregor, both pretty and bright,
And Mamie Geotz, charming, with footsteps light;

Next comes Gracie Chaffin, sweet-voiced and fair,
And then Florence Bradley with queenly air;
While Jessie Newman, a pretty young girl,
With Effie Vreeland, in beauty a pearl,
Sweep past in the march on the waxened floor;
They're last, but not least of the fair twenty-four.

All honor then give to our Company K;
But the story I've told, and further will say
While specially mentioning few at this time
I'm obliged to do this if the story's in rhyme,
And I've hoped as I witnessed their marching to-night
That the future to each one may e'er seem as bright
And be but the reflex of what now appears
As they march down the aisles of the untrodden years;

May to these gems in girlhood a bountiful share
Be vouchsafed of Divine and Omnipotent care:
For by such to this life there is graciously given
A beauteous charm earth has borrowed from Heaven.[1]

Chapter 1

Amazon Rising

Newspapers struggled with how to explain Wyoming's forgotten women's militia known as Company K and Company H. Periodicals often used the word *Amazon* to convey a picture of strong women with ties to the suffrage movement. This practice began with an article in the *Cheyenne Daily Leader* that ridiculed Annie Dickinson, a Quaker woman who earned a national reputation as a women's suffrage orator, when she addressed a crowd of 250 on September 24, 1869:

> *Tonight—This evening the distinguished lecturer Miss Annie Dickinson, lectures at the U.S. Court House. This is quite an event in our city, whose remote situation from the Eastern literary market renders it inconvenient for us to secure the services of many of the notables who abound there. Good fortune has however, given our people this opportunity to listen to one of the most entertaining and graceful orator.*
>
> *We have been accused of saying harsh things about Miss Annie. But we desire to say right here, that on merely personal grounds, we entertain no unkind sentiments towards the lady. As a lady we respect her, are proud of her as a genuine specimen of American womanhood. But when it comes to the absurd question of Female suffrage, then Miss Dickinson, in common with her sister advocates of the preposterous hobby, must come for her share of the ridicule. We will say this of her; Miss Annie is the most ladylike, the best looking, and decidedly the most feminine of all the suffrages. Had she left that odious clique of Amazons alone, she might have been America's*

Literary Queen. But as a gentleman she is not a success. We believe however, that she would make a good man a wife.[2]

Cheyenne newspapers continued to use the Amazon moniker to describe Wyoming's Girl Guard Militia because its members defied convention. The *Wyoming Commonwealth* said:

It is perhaps possible that some who have heard of the now famous Wyoming Girls Guards, think that woman suffrage in this state has revived the fabled race of Amazons who established the empire on the coast of Euxine in the olden times, and that they had taken charge of the military department of the state to the exclusion of the sterner sex. This is very far from the truth.

The constitution of this state makes women subject to all the duties and clothes them with all the power usually conferred upon the male citizens in all of the states, with the single exception that they are exempt from military duty.[3]

The inspiration for Wyoming's forgotten women's militias can be traced back to a little green book written by Lieutenant Hugh Reed in 1883, titled *Broom Tactics, or Calisthenics in a New Form for Young Ladies.* An advertisement said it was "a very desirable book for young ladies wishing to learn something of military drill." The book was more than a novelty, as society was influenced by the military. Women's Aid Societies realized drills and marches could draw a crowd, so they soon formed "broom brigades" to fundraise. The first broom brigade in Cheyenne, Wyoming, debuted at the Strawberry Festival held at Library Hall on June 22, 1883. The *Cheyenne Daily Leader* said:

Eighteen or twenty of Cheyenne's most charming and accomplished young ladies will give an exhibition of their skill and proficiency in wielding this "woman's weapon." During the evening, it is expected they will make a charge on the hearts of the young gentlemen that will be perfectly irresistible and captivating. Tickets of admission to both Opera house and hall for adults, fifty cents; children under twelve years, twenty-five cents. The proceeds of the entertainment will go towards furnishing the new Congregational church.[4]

The Presbyterian Woman's Aid revived the broom brigade in spirit by hosting a military-style drill at Keefe Amusement Hall composed of twenty-one society boys and girls who performed with rifles instead of brooms. One year later, the Presbyterian women debuted an all-female rifle drill team.

Company K debuted on the evening of October 22, 1889, at the Merchant Carnival held at Keefe Hall. Japanese paper lanterns hanging from the twenty-six-foot-high ceiling illuminated colorful banners that graced the walls. Below, a "surging mass of humanity" exceeding four hundred, crowded around sixty-five merchant tables displaying the latest Christmas merchandise. In the background, George Inman and his orchestra played several renditions of "Handsome Ladies in Elegant and Unique Costumes."

The women in attendance were the belles of Cheyenne society who forsook elegant gowns for silly costumes. Francis Hale, the wife of the late governor William Hale, wore a black silk dress decorated with cranberries, crackers and a legend of Ivory soap. She completed her ensemble with some clothespins on a gilded helmet and a mop stick. Jeanette Dewey, representing the Cheyenne Commercial Company, wore a celery- and parsley-trimmed hat and a bright red cashmere dress monogrammed with three "Cs" made of rice, corn and hominy surrounded by dried apples, crackers and clothespins. And Sarah Reel—the wife of Heck Reel, an old-time freighter who battled Indians under the illumination of ten thousand pounds of burning bacon—was dressed to kill with her fishing net hat and necklace of pocketknives. She also wore a cartridge belt and revolver around her waist and carried a game bag containing roast duck and broiled trout.

Early broom brigades in Cheyenne paved the way for the famous Company K. Women's Aid Societies often used the novelty act to raise money for churches.

At eight o'clock, twenty-four "athletic beauties" marched onto the solid maple drill floor in groups of four as Inman's orchestra played a promenade. Reverend Robert Edgar Field, the evening's master of ceremony, introduced the main attraction he facetiously called "Company K."

The capacity crowd sat in silence as Company K stood on an imaginary line with heels aligned, knees slightly flexed and feet at a sixty-degree angle. Each girl took a deep breath and squared her shoulders as she lightly gripped her rifle, awaiting the first command from Colonel Frank Stitzer, a five-foot ten-inch Civil War hero with steely blue eyes and sandy blond hair and mustache. The colonel orchestrated his young charges through a flawless performance of dress and manual drills, flanks and obliques and difficult cross patterns in a performance that was so magical, the *Cheyenne Daily Sun* said, that Company K "became in his hands a fairy machine." Seasoned infantry soldiers from nearby Fort D.A. Russell praised the elite performance, saying, "Such drilling as this company did is seldom seen anywhere." The Company B men's drill team "frankly admitted themselves outdone by the young ladies."

Company K formed a semicircle in front of the stage for an impromptu presentation to Colonel Stitzer. Lieutenant Gertrude Morgan, the sixteen-year-old daughter of former territorial governor Elliot S.N. Morgan, stepped from the ranks and addressed their drillmaster: "Dear Colonel. We desire you and our friends to know that we highly appreciate the instruction you

Company K debuted at Keefe Hall on October 22, 1889. The hall was located on Ferguson Avenue between Eighteenth and Nineteenth Streets.

Company K presented this ebony cane with gold foliate design to Captain Frank A. Stitzer at its debut on October 22, 1889. *Union Drummer Boy.*

have given us. We have often taken your time and often tried your patience. Please therefore accept a slight token of remembrance from Company K."

Captain Emma O'Brien presented him with a "splendid ebony cane with a big gold head inscribed: To Capt. F.A. Stitzer from Company K." Colonel Stitzer "thanked his fair command in the most graceful and fitting terms for their beautiful gift." He promised to cherish it as one of the most "precious souvenirs" of his military career.

Company K finished the evening with an encore performance. Company K members debuting at the Merchant Carnival were Emma O'Brien, Kate Kelly, Mary Davidson, Gertrude Morgan, Lulu Maxwell, Alweine Gloye, Gertrude Ellis, Mamie Horrie, Eva Smalley, Iona Davis, Edna Wilseck, Carrie Ingram, Ada Johnston, Clara Newman, Isabelle Montgomery, Bessie Vreeland, Jessie A. Lee, Ora Cowhick, Mina McGregor, Mamie Goetz, Grace Chaffin, Florence Bradley, Josie Newman and Effie Vreeland.

Chapter 2

Battle of the Sexes

C ompany K's encore at the Merchant Carnival was not a curtain call for the military maidens whose performance rivaled "West Point cadets." Their mesmerizing performance led to additional invitations and sparked a battle of the sexes.

The first indication of gender tension is found in the *Weekly Cheyenne Sun* following Company K's performance for the Grand Army of the Republic (GAR):

> *A movement is being organized among the high school boys to form a company of cadets and Colonel Stitzer has been requested to train the young military aspirants. The male students have for some time been consumed with a feeling of envy and almost despair, as they witnessed the triumphs of the girls guards.*
>
> *Their superb evolutions and perfect drills have aroused the military ardor of the boys and now they propose to get round and make an equally brilliant record. They will have to rustle all over the arena of military tactics to equal their military sisters.*[5]

The lack of physical evidence suggests boys were short-lived in their boast to equal the success of Company K. A study showed that military drill "will not tend to fill a boy with a consuming enthusiasm." Boys needed incentives—a medal or bragging rights. They also needed attention from some of the high school girls who acted as nurses.[6]

A company of boy cadets did exist around April 1890, but military drill failed to sustain boyish interest, and the boys' company, known as Adams' Cadets, only appeared in public once at a military review conducted by General Russell Algers, commander of the Grand Army of the Republic:

> *A word should be said here in regard to Captain Adams' cadets, a company of boys from 12 to 16 years of age. Although the company was but recently formed and has had but little drill the little fellows carried themselves with a military bearing that was admirable and executed the orders given them with much skill and readiness. Captain Adams has succeeded remarkably well with the cadets and with them deserves great credit for their fine appearance yesterday.*[7]

Company K, in contrast, was made up of seasoned veterans with five public appearances to date. Wyoming held a statehood rally on October 30, 1889, to vote for the Wyoming constitution. The *Cheyenne Sun* newspaper suggested sending Company K to Washington "to show our statesmen what the girls can do in the militia service. As a good, graceful and lovely lobbyist they would make congressmen and senators surrender at discretion and admit that the women of Wyoming at least were deserving of statehood."[8]

Wyoming ratified a constitution on November 5, 1889, that included a provision for all male and female residents to vote and hold office. The delegates failed, however, to pass an amendment allowing women to serve in the militia.

Three days later, Company K performed for a group of Civil War veterans at Keefe Hall in Cheyenne. The evening performance for the Grand Army of the Republic commenced at seven o'clock with a call to order by General Joseph Washington Fisher. Wesley Philemon Carroll, a local justice of the peace, recited a solemn tribute to recently departed members. Captain Nicholas J. O'Brien, a decorated Indian War hero, entertained the crowd with his quick Irish wit and a recounting of the Battle of Waterloo against Sitting Bull near Fort Sedgwick, Nebraska. He then yielded the floor to his daughter, Captain Emma O'Brien, and the "already famous Company K Girl Guards." The military maidens earned accolades from Seventeenth Infantry officers from nearby Fort D.A. Russell who proclaimed their performance as "perfect."

The *Weekly Sun* said: "Col. Stitzer's Co. K Guards take the cake—or would if there was any in sight. Seriously, they are the finest piece of composite mechanism to be found in the country."[9]

The *Cheyenne Daily Sun* said:

> *Their action and drill on this occasion was something admirable. In precision, skill and grace their performance was even more beautiful and perfect than when they first appeared at the Merchant's Carnival. The whole company was to the beholder a perfectly controlled machine in motion and the "poetry of motion at that."*[10]

Wyoming's statehood aspirations were dealt a blow in the new year when a statehood bill introduced on January 13, 1890, did not get out of committee. This minor setback did not deter Company K from donning uniforms once again for back-to-back performances at another Grand Army of the Republic banquet in Cheyenne and a church benefit in Greeley, Colorado. The *Cheyenne Sun* continued to praise the damsels of drill, saying, "The skill and precision with which every order is carried out might well be emulated by the best drill regulars."[11] The newspaper said Company K interrupted its stellar performance at the GAR banquet because of the small boys at the entertainment who "as usual made themselves disgustingly noisy."

Cheyenne's women warriors departed the city the following morning to catch a southbound train to Greeley. They were met at the train depot in the early morning hour by a group of well-wishers and a gaggle of boys who followed the "happy and blushing young troop." Colorado newspapers did not report on the exhibition drill fundraiser, but the *Daily Sun* said:

> *A special telegram received by the* Sun *last night says the Girl Guards arrived at Greeley at 3:30 after a pleasant trip and received quite an ovation on their arrival from the crowds assembled at the depot. In the evening they gave a most perfect exhibition drill before a large audience, winning rounds of applause and extravagant encomiums from the Greeley people. All are well and having a delightful trip.*[12]

Company K earned a comparison to West Point cadets and won the hearts of male admirers from Rawlins, Wyoming, who made overtures to Company K to visit their city in the western part of the state. The *Sun* added:

> *Cheyenne has a company of young lady guards who go through the military tactics in a way that would be credit to a West Point cadet. They are giving exihibitions* [sic] *at neighboring towns. Should they come to Rawlins they*

Schools promoted fitness by combining brooms, rings or dumbbells with marching movements. Calisthenics and Light Gymnastics for Home and School *by Alfred M.A. Beale, 1888.*

would be right royally received. We understand the Bachelors club is making overtures in that direction. Did the club know that the girls guards were accompanied by a number of young gallant they would probably withdraw their proposition.

The following members participated at the Greeley benefit: Carrie Ingram, Mary Davidson, Emma O'Brien, Kate Kelly, Lulu Maxwell, Grace Chaffin, Mamie Horrie, Gertrude Morgan, Bessie and Effie Vreeland, Gertrude Ellis, Alweine Gloye, Mamie Hayter, Iona Davis, Jessie Lee, Edna Wilseck, Clara and Josie Newman, Isabelle Montgomery, Florence Bradley, Eva Smalley, Ada Johnston, Minnie (Mina) McGregor and Ora Cowhick.

Chapter 3

Guards of Honor

Wyoming representative Joseph Carey lobbied Congress on March 26, 1890, to pass House Resolution 982 granting Wyoming statehood. Representative Carey, however, did not mention women's suffrage in his speech, fearing it might harm Wyoming's statehood chances. HR 982 was ratified by the House of Representatives the following day by a vote of 139 to 127.

Company K continued to perform, and their popularity inspired young women to form other Girl Guard Militias. Sometime around March 21, 1890, the western railroad town of Rawlins stood up a company of girl cadets who aspired for an invitation to march in the Wyoming statehood celebration. They were followed by another company that organized in Cheyenne some two weeks later.

Company K held a benefit hop at Keefe Hall on April 16, 1890, to raise monies for new uniforms for the statehood jubilee. They charged seventy-five cents for admission that included supper and performances by Company K and the Union Pacific Band. Three days later, Captain Emma O'Brien placed an "official order to report" notice in the local newspapers. The *Cheyenne Daily Leader* and *Cheyenne Daily Sun* from April 19, 1890, said: "Members of Wyoming Girl Guards, Co. K. will report at the residence of Mrs. Wm. Myers, Ninteenth [*sic*] street, at 12 o'clock to day [*sic*], to participate in the demonstration in honor of Gen. Alger and Mrs. Logan."

The order was signed by "E. O'Brien, Capt."

The girls of Company K met at 397 East Nineteenth Street to discuss their appointed roles as guards of honor for Mary Logan, a distinguished member of the Women's Relief Corporation. Logan was also the driving force who inspired Congressman John Logan (Michigan) to sponsor a bill to make Decoration Day a national holiday. General Russell Alger, the other distinguished party, was the eighteenth commander-in-chief of the Grand Army of the Republic.

Governor Francis E. Warren and officials from Fort D.A. Russell met the party at the train depot the following day and escorted them to the fort for a dress review and parade. The official party later traveled to the capitol building for a review of the state militia and the famous Company K.

The *Cheyenne Weekly Sun* said:

> *The grand feature of the occasion was the first appearance of the Girl Guards in a street parade. Before reforming the lines for the march to the depot they gave an exhibition drill in honor of the distinguished visitors. Exclamations of admiration were heard on every hand at the beauty and precision of their movements. Mrs. Logan and General Alger were delighted and could not say enough in their praise. Mrs. Logan thought she had never seen anything so fine in all her life and thanked them most heartily for the pleasure she had experienced.*

Company K formed a line facing General Alger and his party before the march back to the train depot. Captain Emma O'Brien smartly drew her sword and reported to the general as the other members divided into two columns and flanked the official party for the fifteen-minute march. This unexpected military courtesy impressed General Alger so much that he said "it was the highest compliment he had ever received and the only time in his life it had occurred, to be escorted by a company of girl guards."[13]

A brief article in the *Cheyenne Daily Sun* said, "Company K Cheyenne girl guards are the pride of Cheyenne. Their praises are in every mouth and their fame will spread abroad through the land." The *Pittsburgh Dispatch* (Pennsylvania), *Washington Critic* (Washington, D.C.), *Sunday Union* (Sacramento, California) and *Daily Morning Astorian* (Oregon) all carried a newswire report of General Alger and Mary Logan's visit to Cheyenne in their daily periodicals between April 22 and April 29, 1890.

Company H—Cheyenne's second Girl Guard company—organized on April 4, 1890, under Lieutenants George Ruhlen and Edgar Walker of the Seventeenth Infantry at Fort D.A. Russell. The young lieutenants promised that "the girls will be well drilled and are expected to be 'au fait' in military tactics in time to take part in the statehood celebration." On May 15, 1890, Keefe Hall was decorated in a kaleidoscope of red, white and blue bunting and a banner with the company's initial in "pretty letters" that was suspended from the hall's twenty-six-foot ceiling.

Ordinarily, Governor Francis E. Warren, a decorated Civil War hero and Medal of Honor recipient, executed the role as commander-in-chief of state militias. But not today. His stand-in was the Reverend Robert Edgar Field, a "physically delicate man." Company H marched into the hall under the watchful eye of their sisters-in-arms and, with "precision and fine soldierly bearing," formed an *H* on the drill floor. Lieutenant George Ruhlen stepped forward, saluted Reverend Field and presented the company for review: "In the absence of his excellency, the governor, while you are acting in the capacity of his Representative, I have the honor to present to you Company H, Wyoming State Guards, duly mustered into service and determined to stay there till every bachelor in Wyoming has surrendered or left the state."[14]

Reverend Field congratulated the company on its "soldierly discipline and handsome appearance." He said the members would do credit to themselves and the soldierly profession and be worthy comrades to Company K. During the hourlong drill, the girls of Company H manipulated their rifles in the manual of arms drill "like old veterans" and executed platoon and company movement and bugle-directed skirmish drills.

Company H made two unscheduled presentations to Lieutenants Ruhlen and Walker after the applause subsided. Company captain Hattie Argesheimer stepped from the ranks and thanked Lieutenant Ruhlen for his "unwavering kindness, patience and courtesy while undertaking the self-imposed task of directing them in the knowledge and practice of military movements." She then presented him with a beautifully illustrated gift book with the names of company members inscribed on the inside jacket. Company H's other officer, Lieutenant Helen Furness, thanked Lieutenant Walker for transforming Company H from an "awkward squad" of green recruits to a type "of good heroic womanhood." She then presented Lieutenant Walker with a poetry book inscribed with the names of company members.

The scheduled performance resumed with "interesting and picturesque" skits that included interpretations of reveille on a frosty morning, roll call, dinner call, camp alarm, Taps and Columbia receiving young Wyoming. The evening concluded with a dance. Twenty-four girls attended the organizational meeting in early April, but only twenty-two were present at the debut. Company H members present at the debut were Hattie Argesheimer (captain), Helen Furness (lieutenant), Emma Schilling (first sergeant), Adah Haygood (second sergeant), Gertrude Douglas, Mamie Thompson, Dora Adair, Levina Grainger, Mattie Thompson, Gretchen Hermann, Frances Moore, Marie Wedemeyer, Minnie Gape, May Oakley, Maud Post, Jennie Tupper, Kittie Gordon, Mabel Tupper, Bertha Wedemeyer, Mamie Layden, Marcelline Rouleau and Minnie Thompson.[15]

Company H returned to action some two weeks later as it joined in a Decoration Day ceremony at Fort D.A. Russell. Company K also participated in the solemn ceremony, but the mention of it is absent from newspaper coverage because Company H was now the flavor of the month. The local papers said Company H was "honored with a place in the parade and looked hand-some in their military uniform, each one carrying snowball flowers. These young ladies seem to be the especial favorites of the Seventeenth Infantry, and it is understood have been adopted as the 'daughters of the regiment.'"[16]

On this solemn day, a "delightful breeze" tempered the sun's beating rays as the party marched over the uneven prairie to the cemetery. Flags and "many beautiful flowers were strewn upon the earthly mounds of the soldiers' dead," and a bugler played Taps while a detachment of twenty soldiers fired three volleys over each grave. Most of the attending party returned to Cheyenne after rendering honors, but Company H remained on the post for "an elegant reception at the quarters of Lieutenant Ruhlen." They returned to Cheyenne by post ambulance in time for the afternoon parade. Company H later attended an evening memorial service with Company K at the Methodist church.

Wyoming rejoiced when President Benjamin Harrison signed the legislation, making the territory a state, on July 10, 1890. Several prominent Cheyenne women formed a planning committee for the presentation of the statehood flag to Governor F.E. Warren. Wyoming printed special statehood circulars inviting other states and territories to visit Cheyenne on July 23, 1890, to witness "the greatest exhibition of fireworks ever witnessed in the west" and to see the "only thoroughly trained and fully equipped Companies of Girl Guards in the world."

The *Cheyenne Sun* said, "The interesting feature of the parade will be the two companies of Girl Guards in their new uniforms, one company forming an escort for the state flag and the other escorting the statehood car of forty-four young girls representing the states of the union, each carrying a banner and wreath."[17]

Patriotic colored banners fluttered in the warm breeze around the capital city, and new flags with forty-four stars waved from each wing of the

Left: The silk ribbon with customized gold letters and black fringes worn by Mabel Tupper at the Decoration Day ceremony at Fort D.A. Russell in 1890. *Wyoming State Museum.*

Below: The Girl Guards Militia marched from the Fort D.A. Russell railroad station to decorate graves of fallen soldiers during Decoration Day ceremonies in 1890. *Warren ICBM and Heritage Museum.*

A Wyoming statehood celebration circular from 1890 advertising "the only thoroughly trained and fully equipped Companies of Girl Guards in the world." *Wyoming State Museum.*

capitol. Both companies assembled at the corner of Ferguson and Sixteenth Streets at five o'clock in the morning for a final walkthrough of the parade. The morning was chilly, and the sky was filled with rain clouds. Parade participants ducked under wagons and found sanctuary in doorways of downtown storefronts and the nearby train depot as a rogue cloud burst halted preparations. The precipitation was light compared to the storm, described as "one of the most furious rain and thunderstorms ever witnessed," that had deluged Cheyenne the previous day. After the rain, an abundance of sunshine tempered with a light breeze prevailed, allowing the four divisions of the parade to wend through Cheyenne's business district to the state capitol building one and a half miles away.

The parade started at the corner of Sixteenth Street and Capitol Avenue and followed the street railway as it turned east on Seventeenth Street and continued to Maxwell. The procession headed north on Maxwell to Twenty-Fourth Street, where it turned left and continued seven blocks to the corner of Twenty-Fourth Street and Ferguson. Both companies marched in the second division during the hourlong march past a mass of humanity that spilled over the boundaries of the city park into overflowing streets.

At the capitol, Company K assembled behind the speakers' platform for the presentation of the statehood flag by Wyoming's women to Governor Francis E. Warren. The official ceremony began with an invocation by the Reverend J.Y. Cowhick, who asked for an outpouring of blessing for the young state that it might produce "grand men and women." The reverend then yielded the speaker's platform to Theresa Jenkins, a notable champion who tirelessly lobbied for the inclusion of the suffrage clause in the Wyoming

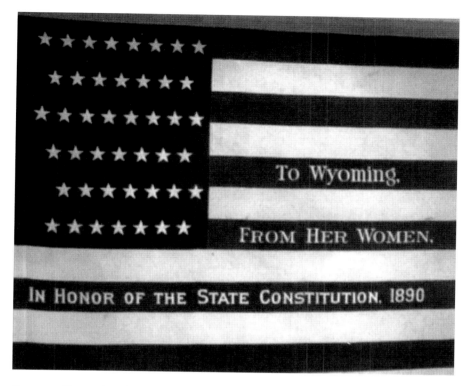

Company K served as the guards of honor to this forty-four-star flag presented to Governor Francis E. Warren at the Wyoming statehood parade. *Wyoming State Museum.*

constitution. In a clear and forceful voice heard some four blocks away, Jenkins delivered the "most eloquent speech" of the day. The speech included a tribute to Company K: "And this young girl guard of honor, picked from the flowers of the state, who to-day have walked through the dusty streets that they might be beside this beloved flag, may well emulate these examples, preferring ever to sacrifice personal comfort to duty and pride to patriotism."

In its last act as the nation's first Girl Guard militia, Company K queued up for a final three-quarter-mile march to Seventeenth Street and Ferguson, where it officially disbanded. The *Wyoming Commonwealth* said of Company K's career, "They were certainly a unique and attractive feature whenever they have graced any public assembly with their delightful presence, and they retire from public life with the very best wishes of all good people who have watched their lady-like and dignified bearing while performing their arduous duties."[18]

Official statehood photograph of Company H taken at the south entrance to the state capitol in Cheyenne on July 23, 1890.

The following members are recorded in the statehood program as serving as Company K officers: Captain Emma O'Brien, First Lieutenant Gertrude Morgan and Second Lieutenant Kate Kelly. The program listed the following women as privates in Company K: Bertha Spoor, Margaret Cahill, Alweine Gloye, Iona Davis, Eva Smalley, Jessie Recker, Belle Smalley, Sadie Bristol, Ada Johnston, Margaret Moore, Carrie Ingram, Edna Wilseck, Clara Newman, Bessie Vreeland, Jessie Lee, Mamie Goetz, Mina McGregor, Isabelle Montgomery, Ora Cowhick, Vilette Houghton, Josie Newman, Leah Ringolsky, Florence Bradley and Effie Vreeland.

Lieutenant Ruhlen was promoted and transferred in August 1890, but Company H continued to win the hearts and accolades of an adoring public as it performed post-statehood at a dress drill and hop on September 5. The benefit "attracted a large attendance, including many prominent society people." The *Cheyenne Daily Leader* said, "The Girl guards drilled splendidly, under the direction of Capt. Hattie Argesheimer, and the hop was most enjoyable. The flower and lemonade booths did well."[19]

This is the last known performance by the "daughters of the Seventeenth Infantry." Company H was invited to perform at the state fair in Kansas City, Missouri, "if the proper arrangements are made." The lack of newspaper coverage suggests that Company H did not participate in the state fair held on October 1, 1890.

The famous Wyoming Girl Guard Militia became the Wyoming forgotten militia in the years that followed. Some fifty years after the historic event, May (Oakley) Leffler donated her copy of the photograph of Company H at statehood to the Wyoming State Archives in 1940. She identified Company H members as: (1) Hattie Argesheimer, (2) Emma Schilling, (3) Minnie Gape, (4) Gertrude Douglas, (5) Jennie Tupper, (6) Mamie Thompson, (7) Mabel Tupper, (8) Levina Granger, (9) Bertha Wedemeyer, (10) Mattie Thompson, (11) Mamie Layden, (12) Gretchen Hermann, (13) Marcelline Rouleau, (14) May Oakley, (15) Minnie Thompson, (16) Maud Post, (17) Adah Haygood, (18) Maria Wedemeyer and (19) Helen Furness. The statehood program listed Private Kittie Gordon, but she is not present in the photograph. Two other members, Dora Adair and Frances Moore, are not pictured because they left the company before the statehood parade.

Chapter 4

Girl Guard Trivia

WHO ARE THE WOMEN IN THE COMPANY K PHOTOGRAPHS?

The Wyoming Historical Society featured a sidebar of the Wyoming Girl Guard Militia in its publication *The Annals of Wyoming* in 1965 to commemorate Wyoming's diamond jubilee as a state. The seventy-fifth-anniversary publication featured the photograph donated by May (Oakley) Leffler, a few sentences about the company's history and the names of Company H members. The publication also lists names of Company K members who participated in the historic event but said no pictures of the company has been found to date.

One of the greatest achievements of this project is identifying the members in the Company K photograph taken the day before the statehood parade and in the official statehood photograph taken in front of the capitol. The statehood program published by the Woman's Executive Committee featured a Company K roster with the following names (alphabetized by author): Florence Bradley, Sadie Bristol, Margaret Cahill, Ora Cowhick, Iona Davis, Alveine (Alweine) Gloye, Mamie Goetz, Vilette Houghton, Carrie Ingram, Ada Johnston, Kate Kelly, Jessie Lee, Mina McGregor, Isabelle Montgomery, Margaret Moore, Gertrude Morgan, Clara Newman, Josie Newman, Emma O'Brien, Leah Ringolsky, Belle Smalley, Eva Smalley, Bertha Spoor, Bessie Vreeland, Effie Vreeland and Edna Wilseck.

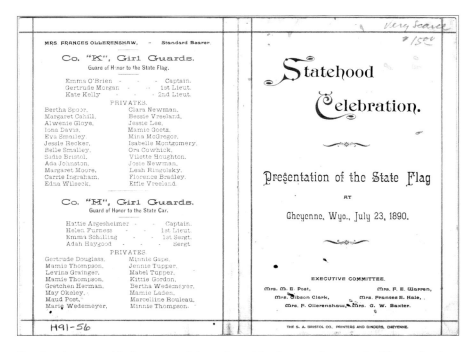

Statehood rosters with the names of the society girls who served as guards of honor for the statehood flag and car on July 23, 1890.

It is interesting to note the official Company K roster printed on the official statehood celebration program does not match the women in the guards of honor photograph taken in City Park or in the official statehood photograph. The women in the photographs also differ.

The photograph of the girls of Company K relaxing on a grassy field (pages 38–39) was taken by Carl Eitner. It has a hand-lettered inscription: "Company K, Guard of Honor to the State Flag. Taken July 22nd 1890." Three names of the twenty-five women—Lulu Maxwell, front row, far left; Gertrude Ellis, front row, third from right; and Grace Chaffin, back row, third from right—do not appear on the statehood roster. Four women on the statehood roster—Carrie Ingram, Margaret Moore, Leah Ringolsky and Bertha Spoor—are not pictured.

Company K members are, front row, from left: Lula Maxwell, Kate Kelly, Bessie Vreeland, Effie Vreeland (reclining), Edna Wilseck, Jessie Recker, Gertrude Ellis, Isabelle Montgomery and Jessie Lee; middle row, from left: Gertrude Morgan, Emma O'Brien and Ada Johnston; back row, from left: Josie Newman, Clara Newman, Eva Smalley, Belle Smalley, Sadie Bristol,

Margaret Cahill, Florence Bradley, Mina McGregor, Mamie Goetz, Iona Davis, Grace Chaffin, Ora Cowhick and Alweine Gloye.

Company K members in the statehood photograph (pages 40–41) are Emma O'Brien, front; first step: Gertrude Morgan; second step, from left: Kate Kelly, Bessie Vreeland, Jessie Recker, Lula Maxwell, Clara Newman, Isabelle Montgomery, Edna Wilseck and Effie Vreeland; middle row, from left: Ora Cowhick, Alweine Gloye, Josie Newman, Ada Johnston, Grace Chaffin, Eva Smalley and Jessie Lee; top step, from left: Margaret Cahill, Vilette Houghton, Sadie Bristol, Florence Bradley, Mina McGregor, Mamie Goetz and Iona Davis. Frank A. Stitzer is pictured in the upper left inset.

Gertrude Ellis, who is pictured in the guard of honor photograph taken the prior day, is not in the statehood photograph. Also missing are Carrie Ingram, Margaret Moore, Leah Ringolsky and Bertha Spoor.

WHERE DID THE COMPANIES GET THEIR NAMES?

Indications are that the "facetious" Reverend Robert Edgar Field nicknamed the group "Company K" because of their youth. The majority of members were between the ages of twelve and eighteen years old, so essentially, they were a company of K(ids). Frank A. Stitzer served with the Forty-Eighth Volunteer Pennsylvania Infantry, Company K, during the Civil War, but this group name does not appear to honor that service. Company H was named to correspond alphabetically with the Seventeenth Infantry units stationed at Fort D.A. Russell.

WHY WAS COMPANY H INVITED TO THE STATE FAIR IN KANSAS CITY?

Politics. The whole history of the Wyoming Girl Guard Militia revolved around politics. Indications are that Company H was invited to the state fair in Kansas City, Missouri, to support Thomas Moonlight's campaign for Congress in 1890. Moonlight was stationed at Fort Laramie during the Civil War and was later appointed Wyoming territorial governor from 1887 to 1889. He later returned to Kansas.

Company K relaxes on a grassy field between the state capitol and City Park. The photograph was taken on July 22, 1890.

Official statehood photograph of Company K taken at the south entrance to the state capitol in Cheyenne on July 23, 1890.

HOW DID THE WEATHER RAIN
ON THE GIRL GUARDS' PARADE?

A brief article in the *Cheyenne Daily Sun* from July 20, 1890, said, "The Girl Guards were to be photographed yesterday for the artists of *Frank Leslie's Illustrated* of New York but the business had to be postponed." *Frank Leslie's Illustrated* carried a brief paragraph about Wyoming's statehood admission in its August 9, 1890 issue, but the article did not mention the Girl Guards.

SIBLING RIVALRY AND OTHER RELATIONSHIPS

The Girl Guards were a family affair. Belle and Eva Smalley and Bessie and Effie Vreeland were sisters and members of Company K. Jennie and Mabel Tupper and Bertha and Marie Wedemeyer were sisters and members of Company H. Margaret and Frances Moore's sibling rivalry extended to the military arena. Margaret was a member of Company K, and her sister was a member of Company H. Company K members Kate Kelly and Lulu Maxwell were cousins. Clara Newman was the mother of Josie Newman, and both were Company K members.

ODDS AND ENDS

Lulu Maxwell attended all of Company K's performances even though she lived some forty-five miles away in Fort Collins, Colorado.

Dora Adair is the only Girl Guard member who became a fugitive.

The Wyoming Girl Guard Militia was never "mustered into service." Some of the members were too young to meet the minimum age requirement for enlistment, and the Wyoming constitution exempted women from military service.

Chapter 5

Tactical Differences

A misconception about the Wyoming Girl Guard Militia is they just "marched" in the statehood parade. That's boring. The companies were more than pretty power-walking parade participants—they were the "only fully trained companies of Girl Militias in the nation." Company K trained in the same civic tactics used by the Knights of Pythias Uniform Rank. The foundation of instruction included basic alignments, orders, movements and marching as individuals and then as squads of four. It appears Company K mastered the forty-three plate movements found in the *Knights of Pythias Drill Tactics and Manual* authored by Brigadier General James Carnahan and Second Lieutenant William Hamilton.

In comparison, Company B, a men's drill team of the Wyoming National Guard, was mustered into service in 1888, but it did not achieve the prominence of Company K. A *Cheyenne Weekly Sun* article was not kind in its assessment of the men's abilities:

> *Company B, Cheyenne guards, will be a year old the first of next month. The company, at that time, will find itself out of debts, with uniforms and equipments, thoroughly organized and with a good start towards that standard of military perfection laid down in Upton and cracked up the regular army troops. All of this has been accomplished by hard work and it is pleasant to note that the attendance at weekly drills is very good and the interest manifested in the company shows no wane. Friday night the guards will have a dress drill and ball at the armory. Tickets cost $1 and are for sale by members. Four men constitute the awkward squad.*[20]

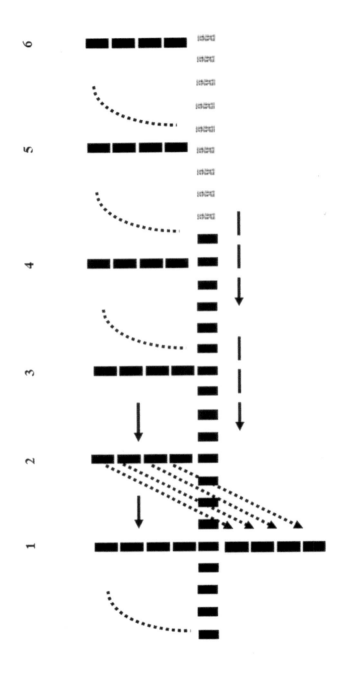

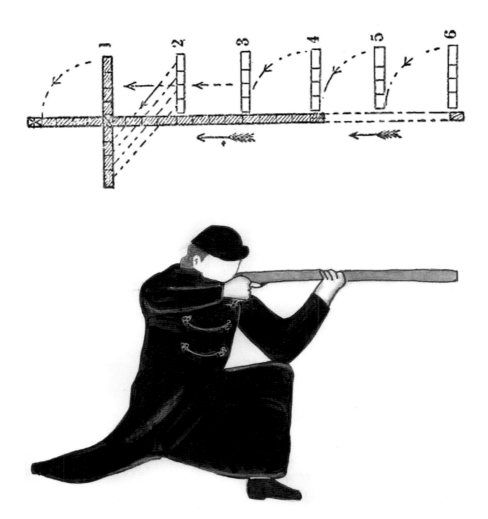

Top: Company K performed the St. Andrew's Cross at its debut on October 22, 1889. Knights of Pythias Complete Drill Manual, *1882*.

Bottom: Company H was trained in skirmish drills, which led to rumors that they were "ready for war." *Dan Lyon*.

Opposite: One of the many drill movements performed by Company K. Knights of Pythias Complete Drill Manual, *1882*.

3. Reveille.

Company H drilled to verbal, silent and bugle commands. Reed Infantry Manual.

The men's team drilled three times a week, but it is unclear how often the Wyoming Girl Guard Militia trained. Indications are that Company K had at least a month to prepare for its debut. A two-sentence article in the *Cheyenne Weekly Sun*, dated September 19, 1889, said, "The ladies of the Presbyterian church have a new entertainment in preparation. It is called a 'Merchants Carnival.'" Company K may have also had the opportunity to practice during school hours because Lieutenant Hugh Reed's *Broom Tactics, or Calisthenics in a New Form for Young Ladies*, was used by public schools as part of their calisthenics program.

The *Cheyenne Daily Leader* said of the debut: "They moved with the military precision of veterans and executed the most complicated movements without a sign of confusion. All seemed self-possessed and not a balk was made. The best and most difficult figures formed were the Latin and St. Andrews crosses. These and other maneuvers were enthusiastically applauded."[21]

Company H was also a drilling machine, but its training included the manual of arms, marching movements and skirmish drills directed by verbal commands and bugle as the Regular Army.

Chapter 6

Uniforms

Company K had four different uniforms during its ten-month career. Company K debuted at the Merchant Carnival on October 22, 1889, wearing "pretty uniforms of light cream with black collars and sleeves and white gloves."[22] Company K's blouse may have had a black high collar and puffy sleeves that tapered at the wrist. A corset and a minimum of five petticoats were also essential wear for respectable women.

There are no newspaper accounts of the uniform the girls of Company K wore at their second performance for the Grand Army of the Republic event in November 1889 or for their two performances in February 1890. However, Wesley Philemon Carroll, a local justice of the peace and prolific poet gives a clue in the opening lines of his poem "The Girl Guards": "Have you seen our 'Girl Guards,' known as Company K? With their miniature muskets and caps of gray!" Carroll was a member of the Grand Army of the Republic, and his Girl Guard poem was printed in the *Cheyenne Weekly Sun* on February 20, 1890.

Members of Company K wore a third uniform when General Russell Alger and Mrs. John Logan visited Cheyenne on April 20, 1890. The *Cheyenne Weekly Sun* said they wore "natty white costumes, blue capes and fatigue caps."

The company's fourth uniform is the familiar gray uniform with chevrons worn in the official statehood photograph. Company K held a drill and hop at Keefe Hall on April 15, 1890, to purchase uniforms for the statehood celebration.[23]

Left: A rendering of the cream-colored blouse with black collar and sleeves worn by the girls of Company K at their debut at the Merchant Carnival on October 22, 1889. *Dan Lyon.*

Right: A rendering of the white uniform and blue cape worn by Company K for General Russell Alger's visit on April 20, 1890. *Dan Lyon.*

Anna Fosdick, older sister of Company H captain Hattie Argesheimer, caused some confusion as to the true color of the uniforms Company K wore in the statehood parade on July 23, 1890. In her recollection of pioneer life, she told officials from the Works Progress Administration in 1937 (discrepancies are in bold):

> *My sister, Hattie, took part in the Wyoming statehood parade.* **She was Captain of Company K,** *one of the two companies of girl-guards participating.* **K company was trained by Captain Rulah and Lieutenant Walker of Fort Russell.** *The guards were Cheyenne girls and enough friendly rivalry existed between the two companies, H and K, to keep them on their toes.* **In the parade Company K stepped proudly in uniforms of black broadcloth with black military caps.**[24]

The *Cheyenne Daily Sun*, in a poor job of fact checking, misidentified Company H as the company "out last evening in full force at Truckey's 'gents' furnishing house to have their head measure for uniform caps which

Company K's second uniform was a gray dress and kepi.

Mr. Truckey is to supply the company." It was Company K that purchased the kepis from Truckey's with the proceeds from the April hop.

A *Cheyenne Daily Sun* article gave the following description of the uniform and kepi Company K ordered: "Color is to be grey to correspond with their uniforms suits and is in style like the ordinary United States fatigue cap. The girls will present a natty appearance when they get fully rigged out."[25]

Further evidence that Company K purchased new uniforms is found in a *Cheyenne Daily Sun* article from May 31, 1890, where the girls of Company K appeared at the Decoration Day exercise at Fort D.A. Russell for the first time in their elegant new dress uniforms, "eliciting much

admiration on elegant costume and fine military bearing." This uniform consisted of a tight-fitting gray wool double-breasted bodice with a slightly puffy sleeve and a high collar. The collar had a hook closure and two rows of buttons. Company K's uniform was adorned with chevrons made from scarlet ribbons folded in a "V-shape." The ribbon was slit at each end and secured behind the buttons. A bustle skirt completed the uniform.

The company's cap was a circular gray kepi with a double-corded chin strap and a brass letter *K*. Captain Emma O'Brien and Lieutenant Gertrude Morgan wore epaulets, but Second Lieutenant Kate Kelly and enlisted personnel did not wear rank. The senior officers also wore red enameled or patent leather belts with silver thread. The belt measured one and three-quarter inches wide and was fitted with a metal clasp with an emblematic lily of the valley design and the letters *U* and *R*. It also had red leather sliding straps and a hook for hanging a fatigue cap. Enlisted personnel and Second Lieutenant Kate Kelly carried wooden rifles, but Captain Emma O'Brien and First Lieutenant Gertrude Morgan carried swords similar to those issued to the Knights of Pythias Uniform Ranks. The sword had a knight's head pommel with a crouching lion on top and a chain extending from the knight's visor to a cross-guard finial and two phoenix birds and a clamshell.

Members of Company H wore two different uniforms during their brief career. The first uniform was described as "natty new suits of blue." The *Cheyenne Sun* said, "They were clad in waist and skirt or [of] dark blue, nest caps a shade deeper and white belt, making a quite fetching uniform."[26]

Above: The girls of Company K wore gray wool uniforms with scarlet ribbons. Enlisted personnel carried wooden rifles, but officers had Knights of Pythias–style swords and belts.

Opposite, inset: The girls of Company K wore loose-fitting scarlet ribbons folded in a V-shape. Small slits fastened the ribbons behind small metallic buttons.

Company H debuted at the Decoration Day ceremony at Fort D.A. Russell on May 30, 1890, wearing blue wool uniforms and hand-decorated silk ribbons.

The company's second uniform, which the girls wore for their official statehood photograph, is described in the *Cheyenne Daily Sun*: "The new uniform of company H Girl guards is very handsome and receives general admiration. It is a black suit with facings of gold cord dropped. The suits are very neat fitting garments. The cap is a regulation fatigue cap."

The bodice was a tight-fitting jersey with a hook closure. The "cord dropped" is descriptive of an obscure Victorian-era method for fastening garments. This was known as a "throg." The uniform color and design were inspired by a horse-riding habit Hattie Argesheimer wore when her father was stationed at Fort Laramie. "The material used was heavy and usually dark. The skirts had fullness for comfort and length to provide protection from dust for the feet. Since we lived in an army post our habits showed a military influence resulting in two rows of buttons and a fine display of braid across the front of the waist. Our caps were ordered from a military firm for us," said Anna Fosdick in her interview for the WPA.

There are some subtle style differences in the uniforms worn by the members of Company H. Officers in the statehood photograph are wearing a double-strand throg, while enlisted have a single-strand throg. Hattie also

The girls of Company H wore decorative gold-gilded throgs with their black uniforms. Enlisted personnel had a single strand, while officers had two.

wore a white belt, but Helen did not. Captain Hattie Argesheimer and Lieutenant Helen Furness wore epaulets, while some members had blue chevrons on their sleeves. The officers of the company were issued swords, but enlisted members carried brown wooden rifles with a leather butt plate

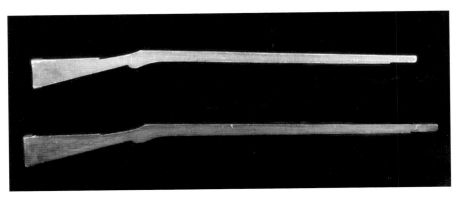

Top: The girls of Company H wore black kepis with gray metal *WSG* and brass crossed rifles and letter *H*. This hat was worn by Jennie Tupper. *Wyoming State Museum.*

Bottom: The girls of Company H carried hand-carved wooden rifles with leather butt plates. These rifles were owned by Jennie and Mabel Tupper. *Wyoming State Museum.*

The girls of Company H wore two-piece uniforms that appeared black but were actually a dark-blue lightweight wool.

attached by small brass tacks. The *Cheyenne Daily Sun* misled readers into believing Company H carried real weapons in the statehood parade:

> *Company H, Cheyenne Girl guards, have ordered an equipment of rifles from Mr. Bergersen's gun establishment. Each member of the company will be supplied with a light and handsome rifle of 22-calibre, and as soon as they are received the company will drill in the manual of arms and target practice until a very high state of profiency is attained in the use of the warlike instrument. They intend to make a reputation as "shootings" and the boys had best be careful and treat them with respect.*[27]

Chapter 7

Biographies

COMPANY K

Colonel Frank A. Stitzer

Frank A. Stitzer is the man responsible for training Company K. Biographical data found in the *Progressive Men of Wyoming* said he was born in Rehrsberg, Pennsylvania, on August 28, 1840. He was the tenth of thirteen children born to John David Stitzer and Sarah Sticknor. Stitzer was five feet ten inches tall with blue eyes and light hair. His obituary in the *Elizabeth Echo* (Elizabeth, Colorado) in 1939 said he was born on July 26, 1840, to John David Stitzer and Sarah Heckaman.

Stitzer attended school "for a limited time" and earned income driving a team on a canal and as a paperhanger until the Civil War broke out. He enlisted in the Washington Artillery as a private but was soon promoted to first sergeant. He received subsequent promotions, eventually retiring at the rank of brevet major. Stitzer served for four years and four months and distinguished himself in the Battles of South Mountain, Bull Run and Antietam.

He resumed his career as a paper hanger and married Josephine Hause on October 1, 1866. The couple had four children: Edgar, Frank, Emily and Arthur (died in youth). In 1869, he accepted a clerical position with the Lehigh Valley Railroad but resigned two years later when he was appointed

Captain Frank A. Stitzer, Company K drill master. He was also addressed by his brevet rank of colonel.

a United States deputy revenue collector in Easton, Pennsylvania, before transfer to Cheyenne, Wyoming, in 1887.

Stitzer worked in the private sector as a real estate agent and insurance salesman before being sued by a businessman in 1890 for the loss of his business after Stitzer neglected to endorse a fire insurance policy. The Wyoming Supreme Court ruled in favor of Stitzer, stating the businessman did not purchase sufficient insurance to cover damages. Stitzer retired from the private sector and was appointed adjutant general of Wyoming in 1890 and superintendent of the Soldiers' Home. During his tenure as adjutant general, he commanded the Wyoming National Guard during a series of historic events. On March 23, 1892, Stitzer staged National Guard troops in Buffalo and Douglas to assist civilian authorities during the infamous Johnson County War. In 1898, the Wyoming National Guard was activated for the Spanish-American War and aided in the capture of Manila, the Philippines, on August 13, 1898. In 1903, he activated and stationed thirty-two troops from Company A in Laramie and Company C in Buffalo at the armory at Keefe Hall to thwart sympathizers who vowed to jailbreak Tom Horn before his execution in 1903 for the murder of fourteen-year-old Willie Nichols.

In 1905, he moved to Laramie, Wyoming, where he continued his duties as adjutant general and purchased the Wyoming Steam Laundry. Stitzer attended a military union in Philadelphia in 1910 but returned to Laramie after Josephine was stricken with paralysis. She died on May 29, 1910, and was buried at Greenhill Cemetery in Laramie. Stitzer became mayor of Laramie in 1912 despite political opposition some two decades earlier when he was campaigning for Francis E. Warren. In 1890, Stitzer and the Republican Flambeau Club were pelted with coal, potatoes and dirt when they marched through the city and chanted "Me and F.E." Stitzer served two terms as mayor, and one of the highlights of his tenure happened on October 4, 1911, when he welcomed President William Taft to the city.

Frank A. Stitzer, *third from left*, and Governor Deforest Richards attend the dedication of the USS *Wyoming* in San Francisco on October 22, 1902.

In 1916, Stitzer removed to the warmer climate of St. Andrews, Florida, where he edited and published the *St. Andrew Bay News*. He later returned to the Rocky Mountain region to live with his daughter. Stitzer attended a Civil War reunion commemorating the seventy-fifth anniversary of the Battle of Gettysburg and made a visit to Pottsville, where he was serenaded by the fife and drum band. He died the following year at his daughter's home in Denver, Colorado, on October 16, 1939. He was buried in the Greenhill Cemetery in Laramie, Wyoming, next to his wife, Josephine. He was ninety-nine years old.

Captain Emma O'Brien

Emma O'Brien was born in Cheyenne, Wyoming, on December 2, 1872. She was the daughter of Nicholas and Emily "Emma" O'Brien. Emma had a younger sister, Fannie, who died on June 2, 1886, from spinal meningitis.

A rendition of Captain Emma O'Brien wearing her gray Company K uniform with scarlet ribbons. *Dan Lyon.*

Emma's life story, like many of the biographies of other Girl Guards members, is best told with an introduction to who her parents are. Nicholas was a deputy United States marshal, sheriff, city councilman, member of the Eighth Legislature and a general land officer who investigated a claim that Senator Francis E. Warren illegally fenced approximately half a million acres of government land between Wyoming and Colorado. Nicholas was an Indian War hero who defended Fort Sedgwick in

Emma O'Brien is buried in an unmarked grave next to her father and sister. Her headstone was destroyed by a tree root after her burial in 1900. *Dan Lyon.*

Colorado Territory against one thousand Cheyenne and Sioux warriors with just twenty-eight men and two pieces of artillery. He also single-handedly dispelled a band of Cheyenne and Sioux braves by swinging a blanket over his head.

Newspapers described her as a beautiful and accomplished young lady. She graduated from local public schools in 1890 and the State Normal College in Greeley, Colorado, in 1898. Emma was a kindergarten principal in Fort Collins, Colorado, until her death in 1900. Her obituary in the *Cheyenne Daily Leader* said she was engaged to a prominent young businessman of Greeley but died of scarlet fever before the June wedding.[28]

Emma is buried in Lakeview Cemetery in Cheyenne, next to her sister, Fannie.

First Lieutenant Gertrude Morgan

Consensus is that Gertrude Morgan was born in Pennsylvania in 1873, but some genealogists say she was born in Lawrence, Kansas, in 1872. She is the daughter of Elliot S.N. and Laura Morgan. Gertrude had a brother, George, and a sister, Lillie. She is recorded in the Wyoming Territorial Census of 1880 as Mary G. Elliot S.N. Morgan was the Wyoming territorial governor in 1885 and again between 1886 and 1887.

Gertrude was a talented pianist, orator and performing artist. She played a hollyhock in a high school production of *The Flower Queen*. She was intelligent and displayed a quick wit, as evidenced in a humorous graduation speech she gave on the statistics of the senior class of 1892: "All members of the class of '92 were born in America. Some of them were of illustrious lineage, one being related to Rip Van Winkle. Average age of class is 18 years and some months, days, hours, minutes and seconds. Height is from 5 feet to 6 feet 2 and total weight 2,462 pounds…"

She married Lieutenant Howard Perry in a private ceremony at her mother's house on August 29, 1894. Perry enrolled at West Point from September 1, 1886, to June 17, 1887, but left for Jennings Seminary, from where he graduated in 1888. He returned to the academy on June 15, 1889, and graduated on June 12, 1893. He was assigned to the Seventeenth Infantry at Fort D.A. Russell from October 1, 1893, to October 1, 1894.

The couple visited Howard's relatives in Woodstock, Illinois, during their honeymoon but did not return to Fort D.A. Russell because the Seventeenth Infantry removed from there before their return. Perry served in the United States Army for some forty-four years and was awarded the Silver Star during the Spanish-American War. He commanded a regiment during World War I at the St. Mihiel offensive and the Meuse-Argonne offensive and served at the Artois (Picardy) defense sector. Federal census records said the couple lived at Fort Sam Houston, Texas, in 1900; in Erie, New York, in 1910; Scott, Iowa, in 1920; and Cook, Illinois, in 1930. They also lived in the Philippines and Hawaii before settling in Sparta, Wisconsin, where Howard served as chief of staff of the Eighty-Sixth Division at Camp McCoy, Wisconsin.

Gertrude died on August 2, 1940, and is buried in Sparta. She was survived by her husband, Perry; daughters Gertrude and Larlette; and son, Perry.

Second Lieutenant Kate Kelly

Kate Kelly was born on January 3, 1872, at the family ranch near Chugwater, Wyoming, located some forty-five miles north of Cheyenne. She was the third child of Hiram and Elizabeth Kelly. Kate had five brothers (Frank, Benjamin, John, William and Charles) and two sisters (Clara and Cora).

Hiram Kelly was a pioneer legend who came to the area in 1849 before it was known as Wyoming and joined the gold rush to California. He worked as an ox cart driver on the Santa Fe Trail between 1855 and 1857. This job proved hazardous to his health, as he was captured by Indians and

Kate Kelly and her siblings stand on a second-floor balcony of the family home located on Millionaire's Row.

almost burned at the stake in 1856. In 1870, Hiram settled near Chugwater, where he and his brother-in-law, Thomas Maxwell, raised Texas-bred cattle. His keen business acumen earned him a small fortune, as he fulfilled beef contracts with forts across the country by being the first to ship cattle by rail from Cheyenne. In 1884, the family moved to Cheyenne, where Hiram built a three-story house and stables west of the capitol building. The house on Millionaire's Row had spacious drawing rooms, a hand-carved black walnut staircase adjoining three floors, several chandeliers, cherry woodwork, decorated brass knobs and hinges, solid plate-glass windows, a stained-glass window on the third floor and a wood-burning fire place with rare wood mantels framed with pictorial English tiles with gold-leaf and Shakespearean themes. The dining room door leading to verandas and sun porches was carved in rare old wood with Norwegian patterns mounted on clear plate glass. The house was finished with floors of oak, walnut, white maple and cherry in multiform designs.

A horse-chestnut tree, apple and pear trees and a white lilac bush grew in the family yard surrounded by a wrought-iron fence decorated with a combination of arrows and tiny tomahawks. Legend has it that the white lilac bushes died shortly after the family sold the home in 1902 because Elizabeth cursed them before the family moved to Colorado. The former family home was razed in the late 1960s and replaced by a parking garage, but the cupola on the barn was reclaimed and now sits on top of a school in Henderson, Colorado.

Kate was described as a "charming young lady." She enrolled at the State Normal teacher college in Greeley, Colorado, in 1890 and graduated with the class of 1894. After graduation, she settled in Fort Collins, Colorado, where she was active in the city's social life. Kate married Robert J. Andrews on April 11, 1899. The *Daily-Sun Leader* said:

> *At Fort Collins, yesterday, at the home of Miss R. Andrews, Miss Kate Kelly and Mr. Robt. J. Andrews were united in holy bonds of matrimony. The bride is a highly-esteemed Cheyenne lady, the daughter of Mr. and Mrs. H.B. Kelly, and a lady of culture and refinement. The groom is a prominent cattleman of Fort Collins. Mr. and Mrs. Andrews will leave at once for a honeymoon tour which will include a cruise on the Mediterranean, a visit to Naples, Rome, Paris, London, Berlin and other European cities.* [29]

Kate died on September 20, 1946, and was buried under the name Katherine K. Andrews on former family land that is now Grandview Cemetery in Fort Collins.

Private Florence Bradley

Florence Bradley was born in Illinois in either 1875 or 1876. She is the daughter of Robert and Margaret Bradley. Florence had a younger sister, Maude, and a brother, Walter. Robert Bradley accumulated a small fortune as the owner and operator of a "famous" sandstone quarry located west of Fort Collins in the town of Stout. He moved to Cheyenne in the early 1880s and became one of Cheyenne's foremost builders.

Florence married Robert N. LaFontaine at her parents' house on June 20, 1900, in a private ceremony conducted by Reverend White of the Congregationalist church. Robert was a general contractor at Fort D.A. Russell between 1906 and 1911. He was also a city councilman and representative and was twice elected mayor of Cheyenne beginning in 1912. The couple had three children, but Margaret is the only one mentioned by name.

Florence died on May 24, 1957, and was interred in the Bradley family mausoleum at Lakeview Cemetery in Cheyenne under the name Florence Bradley LaFontaine.

Private Sadie Bristol

Sadie Bristol was born in Cheyenne in 1871 to Samuel and Ellen Bristol. She had two sisters, Kate and Ellen, and two brothers, Lee and Charlie. Another sister, Ruth Merwin, died at two and a half years old from scarlet fever just before the Wyoming Territory Census of 1880.

Sadie's parents hailed from Connecticut and settled in Kansas until "the grasshoppers came and ate everything but the buildings." Samuel found work as a bullwhacker between Leavenworth, Kansas, and Colorado City, Colorado, before settling around the mining communities of Blackhawk and Central City, Colorado. The family moved to Cheyenne in 1869.

Samuel Bristol operated a printing press for the *Wyoming Tribune* and is the printer of record for the first laws published in Wyoming, including the first women's suffrage law ever passed. He later started his own printing company, binding books in his dining room at 208 East Twentieth Street, in 1881. Samuel served on the city council for nine years and two terms in the lower house of the legislature. Sadie had other relatives with ties to local history. Her uncle General Edward M. Lee was the first secretary of Wyoming, and a sister-in-law, Daze Bristol, was a socialite, an award-winning journalist and the "First Lady of Frontier Days."

Sadie was active in her church and excelled in school, especially in fine arts and geography. The *Daily Leader* said she was able to draw from memory a set of six maps of the United States and a group of states while in grammar school. She was a bicycle enthusiast and said to be one of the first women in Cheyenne to own a bicycle. The *Laramie Boomerang* said, "Cheyenne has a lady bicyclist in the person of Miss Sadie Bristol, who though unpracticed, is daring in the management of her safety. Other city ladies talk of securing machines."

In 1894, Sadie, wearing an ankle-length dress, several petticoats and a corset, bicycled to Laramie, Wyoming, with her brother Charles. The almost fifty-mile trek along the transcontinental railroad crested the summit at 8,247 feet.

In 1893, Sadie matriculated at the University of Denver, where she met William Mains, a law professor. She and William married and moved to Mount Vernon, New York, where William practiced until his death on January 23, 1908. Sadie returned to Cheyenne briefly and stayed with family before moving to Laramie. It was there she met James Jensen, a forest ranger and timber sale supervisor for the federal forest service in Medicine Bow. The two were married on December 22, 1918.

The couple made their home west of Laramie in Holmes, Wyoming.

Sadie Bristol and brother Charles after a fifty-mile bicycle ride from Laramie, Wyoming, in 1894.

Private Margaret Cahill

Margaret Cahill was born in Cheyenne in 1873. She is the daughter of Thomas and Mary Cahill. Margaret had four brothers: John, Charles, Thomas (better known as T. Joe) and Francis. T. Joe Cahill earned a place in Wyoming history as the deputy sheriff who hanged his friend Tom Horn in 1903.

Margaret's parents were Irish emigrants who settled in Cheyenne in 1867. The census records of 1880 indicate the family originally spelled the last name as *Cayhill*, but they adopted the anglicized spelling of their name. Thomas worked at the commissary at Cheyenne depot (Camp Carlin) and was a founder and foreman of Cheyenne's first organized fire department, the Phil Sheridan Fire Company. He was active in the Irish community, a member of fraternal organizations and served in the House of Representatives from 1882 to 1884.

Margaret was active in her church's musical programs and the Cheyenne community. She graduated from high school in 1891. Her marriage to Charles Seaton Fitz was a front-page story in the *Cheyenne Daily Leader* edition of May 24, 1894. The newspaper said the couple married at her mother's house, and they left for their honeymoon under a "shower of rice and old shoes for Salt Lake, San Francisco, and other western cities."[30]

Margaret died in 1946 and is buried in Mount Olivet Cemetery in Cheyenne.

Private Grace Chaffin

Grace Chaffin was born in Cheyenne in 1872. She is the daughter of John and Mary Chaffin. Grace had three sisters, Eva, Florence and Flossie, and two brothers, Fred and Howard. John served in the Confederacy during the Civil War but resigned his commission because of health issues. The family came to Cheyenne as early as 1869, and John found work as a county clerk and ex-officio register of deeds. He left the government sometime during the early 1880s and started a successful floral business.

Grace married Richard H. Wilson, an army officer twenty years her senior, on June 26, 1895, in Cheyenne. The *Daily Boomerang* said:

At high noon yesterday at Cheyenne, Miss Grace Chaffin was married to Captain Richard H. Wilson. The ceremony, which was very beautiful and impressive, took place at St. Mark's Episcopal Church. Rev. George C.

Rafter tied the sacred knot precisely as the clock struck the mid-day hour. The groom is at present Captain in the United States army and acting Indian agent at Fort Washakie, Wyoming.[31]

At Fort Washakie, Wyoming, they became friends with the legendary Chief Washakie. The couple moved several times, living in Huntsville, Alabama; Fort Logan, Denver; the Presidio of San Francisco; St. Michael, Alaska Territory; Fort Slocum, New York; Fort McKinley, Philippines; Puerto Rico; Fort Crook, Omaha; and Fort Logan A. Roots, Little Rock, Arkansas.

The couple had a daughter, also named Grace, who married a soldier named Leslie R. Groves. He became a lieutenant general and oversaw the construction of the Pentagon and the development of the top-secret atomic bomb research project known as the Manhattan Project.

The elder Grace is also related through marriage to food tycoon Duncan Hines. Grace's younger sister Florence met the traveling salesman in Cheyenne and married him in Grace's living room in New York on September 27, 1905.

Grace and Richard lived in Sparta, Wisconsin, until Richard's death. Grace then lived with her daughter in Seattle, Washington, until her death on February 2, 1943. Grace was interred in Lakeview Cemetery in Cheyenne, Wyoming.

Private Ora Cowhick

Ora Pearl Cowhick was born on July 7, 1874, in Bryan, Ohio. She is the daughter of Dallas Roe and Mary Frances Over Cowhick. Ora had one sister, Larue, and a brother, Glenn, who served as Senator Francis E. Warren's private secretary for three years before he enrolled at Columbia Law School.

In 1880, the Cowhick family moved to Cheyenne, where Dallas worked for his brother Oscar Fitzlon Cowhick at Cowhick Dry Good until he opened his own general merchandise store called The Fair. Dallas closed his business in 1898 and served two terms as county clerk and register of deeds. In 1903, he served as a prosecution witness at the Tom Horn trial.

Ora married George Gorton, a pharmacist, at her parents' home at 2323 Eddy Street on July 15, 1899. The couple moved to Crawford, Nebraska, where George operated a pharmacy and served as chairman of the Dawes County Republican Central Committee and a trustee of Nebraska Wesleyan University. The couple had three children: Edwin, Frances and Mildred.

Ora died in 1959 and was buried in the Crawford cemetery.

Private Mary Davidson

Mary Davidson was born in Michigan in 1870. She is the daughter of James and Elizabeth Davidson. Mary had a younger sister, Lizzie, and two younger brothers, Frank and James. Her father practiced law in Cheyenne and was the prosecuting attorney in the infamous Johnson County War trial in 1892.

She was described as a friendly young lady of extremely handsome appearance. She was an honor student and had considerable talent as a singer. Newspapers said she teamed with her sister-in-arms, Emma O'Brien, for a vocal duet of "Nearest and Dearest" at a Presbyterian church benefit at Tanner Hall, and a Fort Collins, Colorado newspaper reports she sang with Lulu Maxwell. Mary was active in the Cheyenne social scene and is mentioned in Cheyenne newspapers attending a Leap Year Ball in "a dazzling white silk dress.

The Davidson family moved to Pueblo, Colorado, sometime in 1892 or 1893, where James served as a judge.

Mary died of typhoid fever while visiting her grandmother in Chicago. Her death was reported in the *Cheyenne Daily Leader* dated June 18, 1893, under the headline "Miss Davidson Dead." The article said she was twenty years old. Other genealogical sources said she was twenty-three.

She is buried at the family estate in Hamilton, Ohio.

Private Iona Davis

Iona Davis was born in Cheyenne in 1872. She is the daughter of John and Ariominda Davis. Her name was also spelled Ione.

She had two sisters, Elizabeth and Cly. Her parents were early pioneers who settled in Cheyenne as early as 1870. John Davis worked as a carpenter and served in the Wyoming House and on the Cheyenne Board of Trustees in 1875.

Iona attended grammar school with rival Company H members Leah Ringolsky and Jennie Tupper in 1888, but she is not listed among the graduates in the class of 1891. Some genealogical sources said she attended school only until the eighth grade. Iona married Norman Wilson on January 22, 1891. The *Cheyenne Daily Sun* said, "The young people are very popular here. The groom is a machinist, and with bright prospects. Mrs. Wilson is handsome and talented. She was educated in the schools of this city."[32]

The couple removed to North Platte, Nebraska, where Iona gave birth to a daughter, Gladys, in 1897. Iona divorced and moved to Los Angeles, California, where she is recorded in the federal census of 1940. She died on December 30, 1966, and is buried in Los Angeles.

Private Gertrude Ellis

Gertrude Ellis was born in Cheyenne on August 29, 1870. She is the daughter of Henry and Adelaide Ellis. Gertrude had one brother, Lemuel. Henry Ellis was born in England but immigrated to the United States when he was ten years old. He settled in Cheyenne in 1868 and operated a successful confectionery and oyster bar called H.H. Ellis Bakery and Confectionery for forty years.

Gertrude was married at her parents' home on November 17, 1892, to James M. Gilmore. The *Cheyenne Daily Sun* said that he was "a gentleman of

Gertrude Ellis and her father visit with a customer at the family bakery and oyster bar located at 110 East Seventeenth Street in Cheyenne.

superior education and refinement. He takes from Cheyenne, one of its most charming and amiable daughters."[33]

James operated "one of the finest ranches on the Laramie plains" near Red Buttes, Wyoming. He is the son of a former lieutenant governor of Massachusetts, and he continued the family tradition of public servitude in the Wyoming House starting in 1888. The *Wyoming Senate Journal* in 1905 said that James and a committee recommended several upgrades at the Soldier's Home in Sheridan, Wyoming, to include steam heat and electricity and the purchase of an ambulance and "three or four milch cows and some chickens."

The couple had one daughter, Helen, who was born in Cheyenne in 1908. The federal census shows the couple lived in Cheyenne until 1930. Gertrude died in Los Angeles on August 3, 1952. She is buried with her daughter, Helen Gilmore Brown, at Penwell-Gabel Cemetery and Mausoleum in Topeka, Kansas.

Private Alweine Gloye

Alweine Gloye was born on December 12, 1874, in Iowa. She was also known as Winnie, Allvein and Alvenie. She is the daughter of Joseph and Catherine Gloye. Alweine had three sisters, Anna, Minnie and Bertha, and a brother, James. The family settled in Cheyenne in 1877, and John farmed and later operated a saloon.

Very little is known of Alweine other than that she attended high school for two years and was a member of the Holmes Literary Society and the Mystic Maze sewing circle. She married Frank Vreeland on June 5, 1901, and the couple operated Vreeland & Stone Wholesale and Retail Grocer, located at 215 West Sixteenth Street.

Frank died on August 2, 1935, and Alweine died on May 1, 1960, and is buried in Lakeview Cemetery next to Frank under the name Alviene Vreeland.

Private Mamie Goetz

Mamie Goetz was born in Laramie, Wyoming Territory, in 1874. She is the daughter of William and Mary Goetz. Mamie had one brother, William. Mamie's mother worked as a laundress in Laramie while William lived in

Cheyenne and worked as a foreman in the *Cheyenne Daily Leader* newspaper composing room. The extended family Goetz were prominent ranchers, brewers and owners of the Centennial Saloon in Laramie. Mamie and her family appeared to have moved to Cheyenne after uncle John Goetz bought partnership in the Star Brewery located on Fifteenth Street.

Mamie married a William Hodshire in the mining community of Anaconda, Montana, on February 10, 1892. The *Daily Boomerang* of June 15, 1894, said, "Mrs. Mamie Hodshire, formerly Mamie Goetz of this city, has been granted a divorce at Cheyenne from her husband on the grounds of cruelty and non-support."

Mamie taught school in Cheyenne after her divorce until her marriage to Edward Edwards on April 9, 1899. The *Cheyenne Daily Sun-Leader* dated April 10, 1899, said, "The bride is a well-known and esteemed Cheyenne lady, who is a residence of a number of years has endeared herself to a legion of friends. The groom is a man of sterling character and exemplary habits, who has been employed in the Western Union telegraph office."

The couple moved to the agricultural community of Beatrice, Nebraska, and then to Lander, Wyoming, in 1930. Mamie died on December 15, 1951, and is buried at Mount Hope Cemetery in Lander.

Private Mamie Hayter

Mamie Hayter was a substitute for Mamie Goetz at the church benefit held in Greeley, Colorado, on February 8, 1890. Indications are she was also known as Martha Griffith.

She was born in Wales on June 15, 1863, and immigrated to the United States and naturalized in 1880. She worked at the Interocean Hotel, which at the time was the premier hotel in Cheyenne, featuring amenities such as bathtubs and flushing toilets. It was also the first tourist lodging in the nation with alternating current and a lobby telephone. The Wyoming territorial government convened there, and the hotel hosted eight presidents before it was destroyed by fire in 1916. Mamie married Edward Hayter in the hotel's parlor on August 25, 1885. The *Cheyenne Daily Sun* described Edward as a "young man of unusual ability and ingenuity as an engineer and general mechanic." Edward opened the Cheyenne Novelty Work at 209 Seventeenth Street in March 1887, offering a variety of services such as locksmithing, bicycle and tricycle repair, electric bells and all kinds of mechanical work.

Edward opened a second business, the Black Front, on Sixteenth Street in May 1887. The *Democratic Leader* of May 19, 1887, said:

> *A large engine has been placed in the building, together with lathes, etc, is probably destined to become one of the leading establishments in the manufacturing line in Cheyenne, at least everything generally included in the novelty line will be manufactured, and in a very short time, Mr. Hayter hopes to be able to employ a number of hands.*

The couple purchased additional real estate in the vicinity of the Black Front in September 1888 for $1,000 but later sold the property for a $250 profit in February 1890 and moved to the agricultural community of Adams, Nebraska, where Edward worked as an electrical contractor. It is believed the couple had three children: Gladys Nelson (born in Wyoming in 1889), Walter Nelson (born in Kansas in 1896) and George Nelson.

Mamie died on April 30, 1944, and is buried in Memorial Park Cemetery in McCook, Nebraska.

Private Mamie Horrie

Mamie Horrie is the daughter of Robert and Henrietta Horrie. She had one brother, Eugene. Robert was an enterprising spirit who is listed in the first business directory in Deadwood, Dakota Territory, selling sash, doors and blinds for R.B. Horrie, Miller, Silkenson & Company in 1878. Around 1880, the family moved to Cheyenne, where Robert raised cattle and sold real estate.

Mamie enjoyed acting and was part of the production of *Cinderella* and *Beauty and the Beast* held on March 1, 1889, at Keefe Hall. Mamie was an original member of Company K, but she did not march in the statehood parade because Robert removed to Rock Springs, Wyoming, to start a lumber business as early as December 27, 1889. The *Cheyenne Daily Leader* reprinted an article from the *Rock Springs Miner* in late January 1890 that said, "H.B. Horrie, the builder, is contemplating the erection of a fine residence for himself, and the *Miner* hopes to be able soon to welcome his family here."

Indications are the family settled in Idaho in later years.

Private Vilette Houghton

Vilette Houghton was born on July 4, 1876, in Cheyenne. She is the daughter of Giles and Lucinda Houghton. Vilette had two brothers, George and Walter. Her name was also spelled Metitte Bloudine and Valette. Her parents previously lived in Central City, Colorado, where Giles erected the first stamp mill to crush rock. The couple moved in 1867 to Cheyenne, where Giles established a freighting business and Lucinda became one of the first women settlers.

Vilette sang and participated in literary readings and graduated in 1893. She married George Woods at St. Mark's Episcopal Church on September 5, 1894, in a ceremony so well attended that the "church was filled to the doors" by friends of the young couple. The couple honeymooned in the mountain resorts of Colorado before returning to Cheyenne, where they set up home at Eighteenth and Evans.[34]

The couple and her parents moved to Denver in 1898 shortly after the arrests of her two brothers, one for forgery and the other for theft of a mail pouch valued at $14,000. Vilette's father died in May 1908 and was buried in his adopted city of Cheyenne. His obituary said he was survived by "Villete Wood" of 57 West Dakota Street in Denver.[35]

Lucinda died in 1914, and she, too, was buried in Cheyenne. The *Wyoming Semi-Weekly Tribune* said:

> *Mrs. Lucinda N. Houghton, a pioneer resident of Cheyenne, died yesterday [at] the home in Denver of her daughter, Mrs. Valette Woods. The body is to be brought here to Cheyenne for interment beside that of the aged woman's husband who died here several years ago. It will arrive Saturday morning, accompanied by Mrs. Woods.*

Vilette's final resting place is unknown.

Private Carrie Ingram

Carrie Ingram was born in either 1876 or 1877. She was also known as Clara Ingram, Carrie Ingharam, Carrie Ingraham, Caroline B. Inghram and Caroline Belinda Haig. She is the daughter of Hank and Carrie Ingram. Hank was a legend in Cheyenne as the driver for the Cheyenne and Black

Hills Stage Line who single-handedly killed ten Indians in a more than two-hour battle near the northern town of Lusk in 1876.

Very little is known of Carrie except that she taught in Cheyenne in 1895 and moved to Gering, Nebraska, after her father opened a hotel in that town. She married a Harry Haig, a prominent rancher, in May 1898. The *Daily Sun-Leader* said:

> *The county clerk today issued a marriage license authorizing the marriage of Henry W. Haig of Gering, Neb., and Miss Caroline B. Inghram, formerly of this city. Miss Inghram was raised in this city and attended our schools for a number of years. Of late she has been teaching in various parts of Wyoming. She has many friends in this city who wish her much happiness. Mr. Haig is a prominent citizen of Gering. He is a man of good moral character and well known in this city. His friends extend hearty congratulations.*

The couple lived on a ranch in Haigville, an unincorporated town located in the Nebraska panhandle (known today as Haig, Nebraska). Harry died in October 1917. The *Wyoming Tribune* said:

> *It is recalled by old timers that Harry Haig, a nephew of Sir Douglas Haig, commander of the British forces in Frances, was at one time a Wyoming ranchman and married Carrie Ingram of Cheyenne. Harry Haig later died and his widow now lives in Nebraska. Their children have grown up and are being educated in the colleges of the east and in England.*[36]

Carrie died on December 14, 1945, in Denver, and her body was sent to Scottsbluff, Nebraska, for burial in the Fairview Cemetery. She was survived by her daughters (Phyllis Haig of New York City; Julia Haig of Nebraska; and Caroline Ferrar of Denver) and a son, Henry Haig of Denver.

Private Ada Johnston

Ada Johnston was born in Cheyenne in 1874. She is the daughter of Ephiam and Ellen Johnston. She had two sisters, Maud and Marjorie. Ephiam settled in Cheyenne in 1870 and became a farmer and proprietor of E.S. Johnston Staple and Fancy Groceries Fruits, Flour, Hay and Grain, located at 210 West Seventeenth Street. He was later appointed a United States deputy

Ada Johnston's senior class picture, circa 1892.

revenue collector in 1897. Her uncle J.A. Johnston was among Cheyenne's first settlers in 1867. Her uncle George P. Johnston earned a statewide reputation as a surgeon of "eminent ability." Another uncle, M.R. Johnston, operated a successful business in Wheatland.

She graduated from high school in 1892 and taught in Wheatland, Wyoming, starting on August 30, 1892, and in Cheyenne in 1895. She married Harry Farmer in a private ceremony on November 11, 1895.

Ada died in 1956 and is buried at the Rose City Cemetery in Portland, Oregon.

Private Jessie Lee

Jessie Lee was born in Cheyenne in 1873. She is the daughter of Judge William and Mary Lee. Mary died after a brief illness on October 26, 1874, at the age of twenty-six. Jessie had one brother, George, and a sister, Lula.

William worked as an Indian interpreter at Fort Laramie in 1858 and moved to Cheyenne in 1867. He served as county coroner from 1884 to 1886 and as a justice of the peace in 1886, 1888, 1889, 1892 and 1896. Judge Lee was among the minority of prominent men who opposed Wyoming statehood. He said he would "move to Alaska if Wyoming became a state."

Very little is known of Jessie's early years, other than that she married W.H. Butler on February 2, 1892. The *Cheyenne Daily Leader* dated February 3, 1892, said, "The bride was becomingly attired in a neat, close fitting dress of brown henrietta, with fur trimmings, and hat and gloves to match. The groom wore the conventional black." The paper added, "A large circle of friends…highly esteem her for her many good qualities of head and heart. The groom is an employee of the Western Union Telegraph company. He is an expert telegrapher, a young man of exemplary habits and those who know him best esteem him most."

The couple resided at 710 East Sixteenth Street until 1902, when Western Union promoted W.H. to the Denver office. Judge Lee's obituary in 1906 said he was survived by Mrs. W.H. Butler of Pittsburgh.

Private Lulu Maxwell

Lulu Maxwell was born on May 15, 1869. She is the daughter of Thomas and Malinda Maxwell. Lulu had one sister, Anna.

Her parents settled in 1860 near Chugwater, Wyoming, when the region was still part of the Nebraska Territory. Thomas raised some 350 head of cattle on "one of the best" ranches between Cheyenne and Deadwood, but he lost his fortune and livestock during the great blizzard of March 1878. Thomas died later that year in November. Malinda and her daughters moved to Cheyenne, where they lived with Hiram Kelly before they moved to Fort Collins in 1882.

Lulu was active in her church and participated in musical productions in the community. She had a beautiful soprano voice, and the *Fort Collins Courier* said she performed a solo of the *Spanish Cavalier* at a Presbyterian church musical entertainment on March 17, 1887. Lulu married Frank Dennis

Abbott, a deputy county clerk, on April 27, 1893, in a private ceremony at her mother's house on Remington Street. The couple had one daughter, Anna May, born in 1900.

Lulu died on January 1, 1931, and is buried in Grandview Cemetery in Fort Collins under the name Lula Abbott. She was preceded in death by her mother in 1913 and daughter in 1919.

Private Mina McGregor

Mina McGregor was born in Ontario, Canada, in 1874. She is the daughter of John and Anna McGregor. Indications are she had two sisters named Mary and Maud and one brother, Dan. Biographical information on John McGregor is scarce, but he did immigrate to the United States in 1887, and the family was naturalized in 1888. Mina's uncle Alexander was better known in the Cheyenne community as an early pioneer who worked at Camp Carlin as a master mechanic. Alexander later served on the Cheyenne city council and owned a grocery store.

Mina was often confused with her much younger cousin Minnie, who was born in 1880. A local newspaper called Mina "Minnie" when she attended the church fundraiser in Greeley, Colorado, on February 8, 1890. Mina was active in church, local and school musicals and literary readings. She taught in Pinebluffs, Wyoming, in 1893 and in Cheyenne in 1895. Mina is recorded in the federal census living in Cheyenne in 1900 as a housekeeper.

Private Isabelle Montgomery

Isabelle Montgomery was born in Doniphan County, Kansas, in 1861. She was recorded on the federal census of 1870 as Ella Whitehead. She is the daughter of James and Jane Golville Montgomery Whitehead. Isabelle had three sisters, Arabelle, Julia and Kate, and one brother, James.

James Whitehead was Cheyenne's first settler, arriving in the summer of 1867. Whitehead opened the first law office in a small tent on the banks of Crow Creek near West Seventeenth Street. He served as secretary of the first city hall meeting, held on September 27, 1867, and was a member of the first territorial legislature in 1869. He is credited with the publication of the first laws of the territory in 1875, and he established the first business structure in Cheyenne.

```
W      Lawyer        15,000    3,000     Virginia                                          X 13  265  216 Whitehead        Belle          15
F      W   at School                      Kansas                              X 14  265  216 Whitehead       Kate          12   F   W   at
School                      Kansas                              X 15  265  216 Whitehead        Ella          9    F   W   at Home
       Kansas 16  265  216 Whitehead      James R Jr.    7    M   W   at School                      Kansas
X 17  265  216 Kuykendall    William       32   M   W   Farmer       5,000    1,500    Missouri
X 18  265  216 Kuykendall    Elisa         31   F   W   Keeping House                    Kentucky 19  265  216 Kuykendall     John          10   M   W
at School                      Kansas                                        X 20  265  216 Kuykendall     Calhoun        7    M   W   at School
       Missouri                                        X 21  265  216 Kuykendall     Willie         1    M   W
Wyoming 22  265  216 Montgomery    Samuel        37   M   W   Farm Laborer                    Kentucky
       X 23  265  216 Whitehead     Willard W     21   M   W   Farm Laborer                    Virginia
       X 24  265  216 Young         Joseph        26   M   W   Farm Laborer                    Indiana
       X 25  266  217 Lyon          Robert        27   M   W   Clerk Dist Court                Scotland        X    X
       X 26  267  218 Moyer         Sylvester L   26   M   W   Policeman of City               Penn
       X 27  268  219 Slaughter     John          61   M   W   Judge of the Police Court  400  200   Virginia
       X 28  268  219 Slaughter     Sarah         58   F   W   Keeping House                   Ohio 29  268  219 Slaughter
```

Isabelle Montgomery was known as Ella Whitehead in the Wyoming territorial census of 1870. She was also known as Isabel, Isabella, Isabelle and Lucy Ellen.

Isabelle's mother, Jane Golville Montgomery Whitehead, died on October 4, 1866, in Nebraska and is buried at Fort McPherson. Isabelle and her siblings appear in the federal census of 1870 living with James Whitehead, but they were later raised by their maternal aunt, Eliza Montgomery Kuykendall, who had three sons of her own.

Eliza's husband, William, served as a clerk court in Kansas before moving to Denver after the Civil War. He came to Wyoming in 1866 to build forts for the government. Kuykendall later established a successful business supplying timber to build houses on the lots James Whitehead sold for the Union Pacific. William later served as a judge of probate; county treasurer; ex-officio justice of the peace; and in the territorial legislature, where he introduced a bill establishing a territorial wagon road between Cheyenne and the Dakota Territory. He also built the first schoolhouse in Cheyenne and served as the first director for Laramie County School District No. 1.

William Kuykendall moved to the Dakota Territory in 1876 while his family remained in Cheyenne. He served in the Dakota legislature and presided at the first trial of Jack McCall, the man accused of shooting Wild Bill Hickock in the back while he played cards at the Number 10 Saloon in Deadwood. Jurors, however, failed to convict McCall in the murder of the former Cheyenne resident. William returned to Cheyenne after the death of his eight-year-old son, Willie, who died on July 31, 1877, after he was dragged for five blocks by a "spirited horse."

Isabelle Montgomery married William Payne Gannett, an employee of the Warren Mercantile Company, on September 28, 1881. The *Cheyenne Daily Sun* said, "The bride's dress was of satin geo d'orse blue, en train, and trimmed with cut steel. The bouquet was of white plush, trimmed with Mirabeau feathers, and the jewels were of pearl and diamonds."

The couple had two daughters: Helen Warren Gannett, born 1883, and Mildred Gannett, born on December 25, 1885. Mildred died from scarlet fever on March 28, 1889. Francis E. Warren temporarily closed the mercantile company to allow the family time to grieve. The family moved to Denver, where William worked as a dry goods traffic manager at Daniels and Fisher Stores.

Eliza Kuykendall, the woman who raised Isabelle, died on December 21, 1898, in St. Joseph, Missouri, and is buried in Denver. Judge Kuykendall died on March 8, 1915, and is buried in Denver. William Gannett died in Denver in 1927. He was buried at Lakeview Cemetery in Cheyenne. Isabelle died in Denver in 1938 and was buried next to her husband under the name Ella Gannett. During her lifetime, she was known as Isabel, Isabella and Isabelle Montgomery; Ella Whitehead; Lucy Ellen Whitehead Gannet; and Ella Gannett.

The couple was survived by one daughter, Helen Gannett, who died in 1944. She was buried next to her sister at Lakeview Cemetery in Cheyenne.

Private Margaret Moore

Margaret Moore, the daughter of Horace Waldo and Abbie Moore, was born in Minnesota in 1871. Margaret had two brothers, Horace and Jared, and three sisters, Eva, Charlotte and Frankie. The family lived at 417 East Nineteenth Street.

Horace was a pharmacist and hospital steward during the Civil War and moved to Wyoming in 1872. He managed store supplies for the Indian Agency, worked as foreman for the *Cheyenne Leader*, served as county coroner and practiced law.

Margaret graduated from high school in June 1890 and worked as a teacher on the south side of Cheyenne in the fall of 1890. She married Albert Eaton Trump, a machinist, on June 14, 1893, in a late evening ceremony at the First Congregational Church. The couple honeymooned in Manitou, Colorado Springs, Denver and other Colorado points before returning to Cheyenne to take up residence. Albert served as a city councilman and justice of the peace before the couple moved to Portland, Oregon.

Margaret died on December 29, 1925, and is buried at River View Cemetery in Portland.

Private Clara Newman

Clara Newman was the wife of James Newman, one of Cheyenne's early pioneers. Clara, the daughter of Peter and Phebe Laborde, was born in Pennsylvania on September 21, 1856. James came to Wyoming Territory in 1879 and worked on the farm of his uncle, James M. Chadwick, before returning to Wisconsin to marry Clara on March 18, 1883.

James prospered as a rancher, dairy farmer, liveryman, real estate dealer, notary public, county commissioner and prospector. The couple engaged in fraternal organizations and the Baptist church and supported many charities.

Clara performed with Colonel Stitzer's co-ed drill team at a Presbyterian church fundraiser in August 1898 and with Company K at the Merchant Carnival in October 1899. Wesley Philemon Carroll describes her in his poem "Girl Guards" as "pretty." The Newman home at 2222 Ferguson was noted for "genial and generous hospitality," which made the couple vulnerable to profiteers. In September 1910, Clara was

J.M. Newman's Livery Stable was located at Eighteenth Street and Eddy Pioneer Avenue. The business closed in 1903 because of the popularity of the automobile.

sued for $10,000 for allegedly assaulting a house guest with a gun, causing bodily injury and "an intolerable nervous condition." The suit was settled for $350.

James died on July 9, 1912, and is buried at Lakeview Cemetery in Cheyenne. Clara died on July 14, 1925, and is buried next to her husband.

Private Josie Newman

A biography of James Newman in *Progressive Men of Wyoming* said he fathered a son, Cecil, who was born in 1883. There, however, is no mention of Josie Newman, who was born in 1876 or 1877. Indications are she is the daughter of James and Clara LaBorde Newman.

Wesley Philemon Carroll described her as a "pretty young girl" in his poem "Girl Guards." She is Josie Neuman in an article about "Prompt Pupils" printed in the *Democratic Leader* dated February 2, 1886. Josie attended grammar school with Company K members Edna Wilseck and

The Newman family home was noted for "genial and generous hospitality." It was located at 2222 Ferguson Avenue.

Effie Vreeland, but she does not appear among the graduates of the class of 1895. Newspapers record she debuted with Company K at the Merchant Carnival on October 22, 1889; performed at the Grand Army of the Republic on November 8, 1889; performed at the Greeley church fundraiser on February 8, 1890; and marched in the statehood parade.

Private Jessie Recker

Jessie Recker is the daughter of A.C. and Isabelle Recker. She had one sister, Sara. The family settled in 1881 in Cheyenne, where A.C. established a prominent medical practice.

She nearly drowned six months before the statehood parade while ice skating east of the city at Lake Minnehaha. The *Cheyenne Sun* dated March 5, 1890, said Jessie was saved "by some of her companions just

Elementary class photo with Jessie Recker (#26) and Company K sisters Gertrude Morgan (#5) and Ada Johnston (#23) and Company H member Levina Grainger (#5), circa 1880s.

in time to prevent her from going down." Jessie graduated with the class of 1892 and worked as a legal secretary and later for the Smith Premier Typewriter Agency in Denver in 1895. She and her family later moved to New York in 1897.

Jessie married Nathaniel J. Rust Jr., a Harvard graduate and prominent businessman, on July 29, 1904. An inscription on a class photograph on file at the Wyoming State Archives said she went to Denmark as a secretary to a Ruth Bryan.

Private Leah Ringolsky

Leah Ringolsky was born on June 20, 1872, in Texas. She is the daughter of Abraham and Carrie Ringolsky. Leah had two younger brothers, Louis and Morey. Abraham was owner of the Cheyenne Loan Office located on Sixteenth Street between Eddy and Ferguson.

A graduation article in the *Wyoming Commonwealth* of June 14, 1891, said, "Miss Leah Ringolsky is a Cheyenne girl, whose career has been watched with much interest by her friends, as in early years she developed a remarkable talent for music, and all through her school course has added to the honors of the class in the assistance she gave in her fine musical programs." The *Commonwealth* added, "She is expected to complete her musical education in the east."

Leah married David Goldstein on February 10, 1904. The *Wyoming Tribune* said:

> *A number of invitations have been received in this city to the wedding of Miss Leah Ringolsky to Mr. David B. Goldstein, at Leavenworth, Kans., on the evening of February 10th. Miss Ringolsky was for a number of years a resident of Cheyenne, where she was noted as one of Cheyenne's finest musicians. Mr. Goldstein is a well-known business man of Taylor, Texas, where he and his bride will make their home after the ceremony.* [37]

Leah died at ninety-five on November 20, 1967, and was buried in Oakwood Cemetery in Austin, Texas.

Private Belle Smalley

Belle Smalley was born in Cheyenne in 1872. She was also known as Virginia. Belle is the daughter of Benjamin and Mary Smalley. She had an older brother, Edwin, and younger sister, Eva.

Benjamin was one of Cheyenne's early pioneers who settled there in 1867. Benjamin hauled freight between Cheyenne and Deadwood and served several terms as county supervisor of roads.

Belle had a harrowing encounter with a steer when she was just three years old. The incident was recounted by her brother, Edwin, in a 1941 edition of the *Annals of Wyoming*:

> *My mother was taking my sister Virga bell, aged three, for a ride in her perambulator, and I, six, was following along. We were going through the prairie to our nearest neighbors, the Robert Bishops, when Smokey, a steer which was known as a "bunch quitter," because he would not stay with the herd, came toward us on the run. Mother saw him coming and called to me to get under the rail fence. We all got under the fence in time to see Smokey gore the little buggy to bits.*

Belle was a member of the Stitzer's Guard co-ed team that performed at a Presbyterian church benefit in August 1888 but did not participate in Company K's debut in October 1889. She married Arthur J. Gereke on April 25, 1892. The *Cheyenne Daily Sun* said, "Miss Belle Smalley and Arthur Gereke, popular Cheyenne young people, were united in marriage last evening. The Ceremony was performed at the Presbyterian church in the presence of a large number of friends. The bride's costume was a rich silver gray."[38]

Arthur worked as a business and advertising manager for the *Cheyenne Tribune* until he purchased the Quick Job Printer at 1717 Ferguson. He operated the venture until the couple moved to Colorado in 1947.

Private Eva Smalley

Eva Smalley was born in Cheyenne on January 19, 1875. She is the daughter of Benjamin and Mary Smalley. Eva had a brother, Edwin, and a sister, Belle. Benjamin is remembered in Wyoming lore as the man who saved his mules during the blizzard of March 7, 1878. Edwin Smalley retold the story for the 1941 edition of the *Annals of Wyoming*:

Snow fell for days and before long it was six feet deep. That was the storm in which we brought some of the mules into the kitchen to save their lives. My father's mule-shed was at 306 East Twentieth Street. The weight of the drifted snow broke the roof of the shed in on the mules and suffocated five of them. We had a rather long lean-in-to kitchen and I remember we cleared out the furnishings and led ten of the mules in there out of the storm. It was July before all of the snow was gone. Thousands and thousands of head of cattle and sheep were lost in that storm.

Very little is known of Eva's early life, but she was described as "handsome with a wealth of hair." The *Cheyenne Daily Sun* painted a fairy tale of her marriage to Ulysses Grant Crandell on February 22, 1892:

U.G. Crandell and Miss Eva Smalley were wedded yesterday, Chief Justice Groesbeck performed the ceremony at the capital. A few intimate friends of the couple were present. The bride is the daughter of Mr. and Mrs. B.H. Smalley and is an exceptionally pretty and bright young lady. She has been very popular in the circle she has graced. Mr. Crandell is a young man who has a good position with the Union Pacific and who is held in high esteem by his many friends. [39]

Eva's fairy tale marriage became a nightmare as details of her divorce played out in the local newspapers. The *Cheyenne Daily Leader* said:

Eva Crandell was yesterday granted a divorce from her husband, Ulysses Grant Crandell by Judge Scott. The cause was desertion and non-support. It is an interesting fact in connection with the case, that the plaintiff, Mrs. Crandell, is the first woman, born in Cheyenne, to obtain a divorce from her husband. [40]

The local papers sensationalized the divorce with a report of the arrest of Ulysses Grant Crandell in Chicago in September 1898. The *Cheyenne Daily Sun* said:

Ulysses Grant Crandell, formerly of the firm of Crandell & Gooderl, dentists at 2600 Indiana avenue, is charged with bigamy by his wife, Marguerite H. Crandell. Yesterday she began proceedings in the superior court for divorce. Mrs. Crandell alleges she learned recently that two years before she was married to Crandell at Hammond, Ind, in 1894 the defendant married Eva Gertrude Smalley in Cheyenne, Wyo., and that a decree of divorce was never issued to him or to her. Sometime ago, Mrs. Crandell says, Grant disappeared, and she believes he left the state after learning of his wife's discovery.[41]

Eva Smalley Crandell married Demerit Brown on January 1, 1896, in a private ceremony, and the couple moved to Gering, Nebraska, after the wedding. Indications are Demerit was quite senior to Eva because Cheyenne marriage records show he was married once before on April 29, 1880. That marriage also failed.

Benjamin Smalley died on December 5, 1915. His obituary said Eva resided in Miami, Arizona, with her husband, William Morse. The couple later moved to San Bernardino, California, where William worked as a salesman. Eva died on August 29, 1954, and is buried in Hermosa Memorial Gardens in San Bernardino.

Private Bertha Spoor

Bertha Spoor was born in New York in 1870. Her parents are Charles and Rhoda Spoor. Bertha had one sister, Inez. Charles supported his family as a carpenter and carried mail between Cheyenne and Wendover, Utah.

Very little is known of Bertha other than that she was an honor roll student and participated in public school recitations. She graduated from high school in 1887. The *Cheyenne Daily Leader*'s coverage of the Merchant Carnival mentioned she wore "an odd, but pretty dress" in her capacity as an agent for J.S. Collins Saddlery.

She died in July 1894. Her brief obituary in the *Cheyenne Daily Leader* from July 19, 1894, said, "Miss Bertha Spoor died at the residence of her parents, Mr. and Mrs. Charles Spoor, in Chicago a few days ago. She was 24 years of age and was carried off by heart disease."

Private Bessie Vreeland

Bessie Vreeland was born in New Jersey in 1873. She is the daughter of John Van Kiper and Anna Marie Vreeland. Bessie had two brothers, Frank and Edwin, and a sister, Effie. Bessie was a singer and a talented artist. The *Cheyenne Daily Sun* said she "acquitted herself with distinction" by illustrating

Bessie Vreeland's senior class photo, circa 1892.

the graduating class of 1892 history "with striking charcoal drawings, each of which was a masterpiece in caricature."

Bessie taught school in Cheyenne in 1895 and perhaps in Wheatland in later years. She married Clarence Thomas Johnston on October 20, 1897. News of the nuptials appeared in the *Wheatland World* edition dated October 22, 1897, but not in Cheyenne newspapers:

> *Miss Vreeland is the daughter of Mr. and Mrs. J.V.R. Vreeland, and is an accomplished and gifted young lady, who has held a high position in Cheyenne social circles. Mr. Johnston is a graduate of Ann Arbor, and is an assistant in the office of State Engineer Mead. He is a young man of ability and exemplary habits, and no doubt has a bright future before him.*

Clarence was appointed assistant state engineer of Wyoming in November 1897 and assistant chief of irrigation investigation for the U.S. Department of Agriculture in 1899. He studied water drainage and rice cultivation in the western states and the South, as well as Spain, southern France, northern Italy, Algiers and Egypt, before accepting a position as Wyoming state engineer in 1903. He resigned in February 1911, and the couple moved to Ann Arbor, Michigan, where Clarence taught surveying and geodesy at the University of Michigan.

Private Effie Vreeland

Effie Vreeland was born on June 3, 1876, in New Jersey. She is the daughter of Anna Marie and John Van Kiper Vreeland. John was a local florist and served as an assistant deacon in the Congregational church.

Effie graduated with the class of 1895 and worked as an extra assistant enrolling and engrossing clerk for the last two days of the Wyoming state legislature that convened on January 11, 1897. Effie married Fred Wilkins on June 29, 1899. The *Cheyenne Daily Sun-Leader* said, "M.H. Wilkins and wife and daughter and son are in this city from Grand Island today to attend the Wilkins-Vreeland nuptials."

The couple moved to Glendale, California, where they were later joined by Frank and Mary Vreeland in their declining years. Effie died on April 3, 1965, and is buried at Forest Lawn Memorial Park.

Private Edna Wilseck

Edna Wilseck is the daughter of Charles and Agnetta Wilseck. She had one sister, Julia, and two brothers, Will and Charles. The senior Charles was a Cheyenne pharmacist sanitary inspector for the Union Pacific Railroad.

Edna graduated from high school in 1895. After high school, she occupied clerical positions at the state capitol and served as organist for the Methodist church. Her brother Charles died in 1899, while serving with the Wyoming Volunteers during the Spanish-American War. Edna married John Edgar Jamison on October 6, 1904, in a private wedding attended by family and a few close friends. The *Cheyenne Daily Leader* said:

> *A very pretty home wedding was that of Miss Edna Wilhelmina Wilseck and Mr. John Edgar Jamison, which took place at high noon on Thursday at the home of the bride's sister, Mrs. Joseph Skidmore, on House street. The vivid red and green of the woodbine which had been woven into ropes, was very effective and in countless numbers the ropes were used, fashioning a perfect canopy for the ceilings of the parlors, and dining room. The mantles were hung with a mass of autumn coloring in the vines and banked with foliage plants. Ferns and palms were grouped about the rooms and the cut flowers were Liberty roses and white petunias.*
>
> *The bride was lovely in a handsome gown of pale grey silk poplin with white chiffon yoke fagoted, and bertha of embroidered chiffon. The skirt was tucked in finished with several rows of gray velvet ribbon. The shower bouquet was of bride roses and asparagus fern tied with tulle.*[42]

The groom was described as "a young man of sterling qualities who reside[s] in Cheyenne, at one time holding a position with the Union Pacific Railroad company." The *Cheyenne Daily Leader* said the bride wore a gown of "navy blue cloth, tailored, with velvet collar and with it was worn a large velvet hat of navy blue crushed velvet" as they departed for their honeymoon at the World's Fair in St. Louis.

The couple moved to Sedalia, Missouri, where John worked as a machine shop foreman for the Missouri Pacific Railroad.

COMPANY H

Lieutenant George Ruhlen

Lieutenant John "George" Ruhlen, drillmaster of Company H. *Courtesy of Kathleen Ruhlen.*

Lieutenant John "George" Ruhlen was one of the two officers who trained the Girl Guards company known as Company H. He was born in Wurttemberg, Germany, on September 21, 1847, to Johann George and Justina Dorothea Sattler Ruhlen. George had four brothers, Jeremiah, Henry, William and Jacob, and one sister, Justina. The family Ruhlen immigrated to the United States in 1852 and settled in Jerome Township in Union County, Ohio.

Ruhlen graduated from West Point on June 14, 1872, and was promoted to second lieutenant in the Seventeenth Infantry. He served frontier duty at the Cheyenne Agency in Yankton, Dakota, between September 27, 1872, and November 19, 1876; at Camp Hancock, Dakota, between June 4, 1877, and August 1878; and at Camp Sturgis, Dakota, on August 27, 1878. (Camp Sturgis was later renamed Fort Ruhlen on August 31, 1878.) Ruhlen taught military science at Ohio State University between 1881 and 1886 before returning to frontier duty at Fort D.A. Russell, Wyoming Territory, in 1886.

During his career, Ruhlen showed a genuine concern for the welfare of the common army soldier. He supported a pay raise for commissary and post quartermaster sergeants and opposed a post alcohol ban. He said soldiers often left post without authorization after Reveille and found their way into town, where they fell victim to unscrupulous saloons that adulterated or watered down liquor to liberate the soldiers' monthly paycheck. Ruhlen said if a liquor ban existed then every post or army camp would be surrounded by "abandoned women of the lowest type" and the "lowest and most vicious class of saloons that sell the vilest liquors."

Ruhlen was promoted to captain on August 14, 1890, and transferred to Washington, D.C., as an assistant quartermaster. He oversaw construction projects and participated in the Alaska Relief Expedition that saved 265 whalers near Point Barrows, Alaska, during the winter of 1897–98. Ruhlen was promoted to major on June 3, 1898, and given charge of the Transport Service for the District of Hawaii.

A subsequent promotion to lieutenant colonel on August 3, 1903, returned him stateside to oversee all new construction work at military posts. Ruhlen appeared before the House Committee on Appropriations on January 27, 1905, to justify a $35,000 construction allocation for a cavalry, artillery and infantry drill hall at Fort D.A. Russell. He returned to Cheyenne on July 15, 1907, to inspect the drill hall construction at Fort D.A. Russell.

Lieutenant George Ruhlen and Ellen lived at Fort D.A. Russell, Wyoming Territory, in Quarters 28 between 1886 and 1890.

Ruhlen was promoted to colonel on February 25, 1908, and served until retirement on September 21, 1911. He was reactivated during World War I as chief sustenance officer for the Pacific coast. Ruhlen died in Tacoma, Washington, on October 8, 1933, and was interred at the Green Lawn Cemetery in Columbus, Ohio, next to his wife, Ellen, who died four years earlier. Ruhlen was also preceded in death by two sons, Charles in 1874 and Herman in 1887. Two sons, Carl and George, survived him.

Lieutenant Edgar Walker

Lieutenant Edgar Walker was one of two officers who trained the Girl Guard militia known as Company H. He was born on June 3, 1858, in Missouri. Walker married Sallie Rice Stringfellow and fathered three daughters, Elise, Sarah and Margaret.

He entered West Point Military Academy on September 1, 1878, and graduated on June 13, 1883. Walker was stationed with Lieutenant George Ruhlen at Fort Totten, Dakota, where he participated in a campaign against the Sioux from December 17, 1890, until January 26, 1891. He was promoted to first lieutenant of the Twenty-Fifth Infantry on February 24, 1891, and transferred to the Eighth Infantry on July 20, 1891. Additional assignments include Fort Washakie, Wyoming; professor of military science and tactics at Missouri

Lieutenant Edgar Walker, drillmaster of Company H.
Courtesy of Thomas Fitch King Jr.

Military Academy; Fort D.A. Russell between June 1896 and September 20, 1897; and quartermaster and commissary officer at Fort St. Michael, Alaska, and Snelling, Minnesota.

Walker was promoted to captain in the Eighth Infantry on July 10, 1898, and stationed in Alaska, New York and the Philippines until January 1, 1899. He was medically discharged on August 7, 1906, for a disability received in the line of duty. Walker taught military science and tactics, civil and mechanical engineering and descriptive geometry at the University of Florida in Gainesville from 1908 until his retirement in 1945.

He died at the age of ninety-six on January 1, 1955, and was interred at Evergreen Cemetery in Gainesville. At the time of his death, he was the oldest living graduate of West Point and a colonel on the retired list.

Captain Hattie Argesheimer

Hattie Argesheimer was born in Carlisle, Pennsylvania, on September 27, 1870. She is the daughter of John and Harriet Argesheimer. Hattie had an older sister, Anna, and older brother, Charles. She also had a younger brother, Harry, who died shortly after his birth on September 3, 1867, in Washington, D.C., and a younger sister, Laura Alice, who was born at Fort D.A. Russell, Wyoming Territory, on January 23, 1876. She died on March 6, 1876, and was buried at the post cemetery under the name L. Argushuimer.

John Argesheimer emigrated from Germany and fought in the Civil War under Union generals George Meade, George McClellan and Ulysses Grant. John Argesheimer was stationed in Washington, D.C., and became a favorite bandleader of President Ulysses Grant. John was later an army bandmaster in St. Louis, Missouri, until his transfer to Fort D.A. Russell in 1875 with the Third Cavalry.

The trip from St. Louis took several days, and trains at that time had little accommodations and no sleepers. The family arrived in Cheyenne in October and thought it the most desolate place ever. Anna Fosdick, Hattie's older sister, said in her recollections of frontier life for the Works Progress Administration that Cheyenne had small frame buildings with false fronts and garishly painted advertisements. The streets were dusty and narrow, and there were rickety wooden walks in some places. "The whole place [was] absolutely unadorned by trees, lawn, or flowers.…Of course, we were not stopping in Cheyenne. We were being stationed at Fort Russell three miles away, but the thought in our minds was, would the fort be any better?"

As the family approached Fort D.A. Russell, they noticed crude wooden frame houses with interiors lined with adobe to seal cracks in the rough-hewn lumber. There was no indoor plumbing, and water was hauled from Crow Creek and kept in barrels in the yard.

Anna said the Argesheimer children attended school with twenty other pupils during the winter of 1875. Despite the bleak first impression, Anna said Fort D.A. Russell was a beehive of activity. Cheyenne citizens came to the post for band concerts, and empty quarters were often converted into dance halls and decorated with flags and bunting. On July 4, 1876, the post held a centennial celebration that included competitive sports such as foot races, sack races and jumping, as well as music, dancing and food. "We children ate far too much than was good for us," said Anna.

Anna said the family was at Fort Russell when General George Custer and his men were massacred on the Little Big Horn. Her mother knew General Custer, and she often spoke of his long, curly blond hair. The Third Cavalry moved to Fort Laramie, Wyoming Territory, in 1876. The army took four days to travel more than one hundred miles, but families made the treacherous journey over rough trail in one day. Anna Fosdick said the trip started in Cheyenne at four o'clock in the morning, and the horses maintained a furious pace throughout the whole trip. She said the carriage swayed violently, throwing passengers in and out of corners constantly. Hattie added to the excitement when she fell out of the stagecoach at one of the changing stops:

> *Lieutenant Chase was in the coach with us. He was returning to Fort Laramie after a leave of absence. He teased my small sister, Hattie throughout the whole day, probably in an effort to liven up the trip for us. Once when she jerked away from him she fell against the stage door which swung open, dumping her on the ground. Fortunately, we were at a station changing horses and the coach was not in motion so Hattie was not at all hurt, but we laughed at the* [speed] *Lieutenant Chase showed in getting out and picking her up.*[43]

The bandmaster's quarters at Fort Laramie was too small for the Argesheimer family, so they moved into larger quarters. Anna said Indian sightings at Fort Laramie were a normal occurrence, but it still frightened everyone when Indians peeked in the windows. Music and dancing were favorite pastimes, and horseback riding was a favorite diversion for the children, even though they were not allowed to venture far from the fort. The children often found glass beads at abandoned Indian graves, and they were fascinated with a sundial on the parade field for its precision in measuring time.

The Third Cavalry returned to Fort D.A. Russell in 1880 and then to Whipple Barracks, Arizona, "to cope with the Indian situation there." Anna said the family traveled across bandit-infested country by train and stage before they reached their destination. The family remained in Arizona until John's death on March 20, 1883. Harriet Argesheimer and children returned to Cheyenne and built a five-room frame house on the corner of Twenty-

Fourth Street and Ransom. The land was later purchased by the Capitol Building Commission on July 21, 1886, so the family home was relocated to the corner of Twenty-Fifth Street and Ransom, where it stood until it was razed in 1981 for construction of the Herschler Building.

Local papers describe Hattie as a woman of beautiful Christian character and "much more than ordinary mentality." She was active in her church and community, and "her life has been devoted to good works." Hattie attended local public schools and the Cheyenne Business College and taught in Salem, Wyoming, and in Wheatland, Wyoming, around 1896.

She married Harry Hodgin on October 27, 1897. The *Cheyenne Sun* article said, "Mr. Hodgin is not generally known in this city, being a resident of the Wheatland country, where he is spoken highly by all who know him."

Harry was from Iowa but in 1895 settled west of Wheatland, where he operated "one of the finest ranches in this part of the state." The couple relocated to Huntington Park, California, in 1910.

Lieutenant Helen Furniss

Helen Furniss was born in Colorado in March 1873. She is the daughter of John and Ella B. Furniss. Helen had two younger sisters, Pansy and Irene, and a younger brother, Edgar. The family moved to Cheyenne in 1874.

John was an engineer for the Union Pacific and a member of the crew that killed a soldier lying on the track between Laramie and Fort Sanders. Ella Bartlett Furniss was active in the Presbyterian church and owned a fashionable millinery business. She supported her family after a bitter divorce as a dressmaker and seamstress, and she sold homemade bread, pies and cakes, salads and ice cream. Newspapers report Ella was among the distinguished guests seated with Governor F.E. Warren on the speaker's platform during the statehood celebration.

Helen was a talented singer and dancer. The *Cheyenne Daily Sun* dated April 30, 1889, said she was part of "the most ambitious musical effort ever attempted by the younger singers of this city." She was among the "group of charming maidens" that glided in dance and sang as sweetly as a flower chorus during a school production of *The Flower Queen*.

She appears to have been one of Cheyenne's favorite daughters. Wesley Philemon Carroll, the author of the "Girl Guards" poem, dedicated the poem "Isle Seventeen" to Helen on her birthday. The *Wyoming Commonwealth* singled her out from her Company H peers with a special mention in its

October 12, 1890 edition: "Miss Helen Furniss, of Cheyenne, Wy. T., is the first lieutenant of the only feminine company of regular state militia in the United States."

The *Norristown Herald* in Pennsylvania said, "Wyoming has a military company composed of women and commanded by Helen Furniss, of Cheyenne. The name of the captain sounds hot enough to be at the head of a fireman's company."

Helen studied botany at the University of Wyoming in the fall of 1891, and the Department of Botany reported she successfully grew a rare *Lathyrus ornatus* native to the eastern base of the Rocky Mountains. Helen married Lewis C. Rice in a private ceremony at her mother's house at Nineteenth and Capitol on October 19, 1892. The groom was an electrical engineer from Kansas City, Missouri, and described as "an expert in his calling" and a very "pleasant and genial young man." The *Cheyenne Daily Sun* said:

> *Miss Helen Furniss, the bride, needs no extended notice in a Cheyenne Paper. She was reared here and numbers her friends by the score. They all unite in congratulating Mr. Rice for his good judgment in seeking and his good luck in obtaining her hand and heart. The young folks will spend a few days with their friends in Cheyenne and will then leave for their future Home in Kansas City.*[44]

The final mention of Helen is a federal census record in 1910 that states Helen and John Rice lived in Cheyenne with Ella Furniss.

First Sergeant Emma Schilling

Emma Rose Schilling was born on October 15, 1876. She is one of eight children of George and Wilhelmena Schilling. George was a native of Germany who moved in 1882 to Cheyenne, where he plied the trades of carpenter and cabinetmaker. George died on January 8, 1890, so he was not able to see his daughter march in the historic statehood parade.

Emma was an original member of the Stitzer Guards co-ed team that performed at a Presbyterian church fundraiser at Keefe Hall in August 1898, but she did not join Company K, as did many of the young women from the early company. She married Boyd Kirk in a private ceremony on September 4, 1901. The groom was from a well-known ranching family in

Rawlins, Wyoming, and employed by the Union Pacific Railroad. He later worked as an engineer for the electric lighthouse in Rawlins.

The couple was married for a little more than a year until Boyd was electrocuted when he contacted a dynamo and "received the full force of 2,200 volts" on September 27, 1902. The accident caused a power outage in Rawlins. Emma returned to Cheyenne and found solace in church and charitable work. She died in Denver, Colorado, on April 28, 1915, following an operation. Emma is buried next to her husband in the Rawlins Cemetery.

Sergeant Adah Haygood

Adah Bishop Haygood was born in Cheyenne on February 15, 1873. She is the daughter of Allen and Saphronia Haygood. Adah had five brothers, Allen, Arthur, Theodore, Walter and Wesley, and three sisters, Alzada, Bertha and Mary. Bertha died in infancy in 1878, and Walter died in August 1890.

Adah was counted twice on the Wyoming Territorial Census in 1880. She is counted as a four-year-old living with grandparents John and Martha Bishop and as a nine-year-old living with her parents.

The elder Allen worked as a farmer, contract mail carrier, government freighter and agricultural equipment salesman in Kansas before moving to Wyoming in 1871. He ranched near Granite Canyon and Lone Tree and carried mail between Granite Canyon and Virginia Dale, Colorado.

Adah married Oliver R. Bryan in a private ceremony at her grandmother's house on May 6, 1896. The *Wyoming Tribune* said:

> *Mrs. Bryan is the daughter of Mr. and Mrs. A.W. Haygood of Granite Canon, and a sister of the two boys who were blown up and badly injured by dynamite at Granite Canon a few weeks ago. She has been assisting her grandmother, Mrs. Bishop, in her millinery store on Seventeenth street for sometime past, and during her residence here has made a large number of friends. Mr. Bryan is a well-known mail clerk and is universally liked and respected.*

The couple had a son, Richard Allen Bryan. Adah filed for divorce seven and a half years later for desertion and non-support. She later married William Boyce, the son of a prominent rancher from Box Elder Creek, Wyoming. The couple moved to San Bernardino, California, where Adah died on February 24, 1955. She is buried at Hillside Memorial Park.

Private Dora Adair

Dora Adair was born in Bellevue, Colorado, in 1874. She is the daughter of Isaac and Virginia Ann Shores Adair. Dora had one sister, Lora, and a brother, Gilbert.

Isaac was born in Ohio and moved in 1860 to the Denver area, where he worked as an overland freighter, hauling from the Missouri River to Oregon, and he supplied ties and timber for the construction of the Union Pacific Railroad as it moved across the frontier. Isaac married Virginia Anna Shores in January 1870, and the couple lived in Cheyenne but ranched in the Upper Box Elder canyon in northern Colorado.

All the members of the Wyoming Girl Guard Militia were socialites with the family reputation to uphold. Dora was not an exception. Newspapers described her as a "most attractive girl" who was educated in Cheyenne public schools. Dora "enjoyed the best associations in society" and was accorded all the advantages of pleasure and culture that prosperity could afford—until the family experienced a reversal in fortune. Dora's strong will and turbulent life played out in local and regional newspapers.

The saga of Dora Adair began in late February 1891 when she ran away at age sixteen. Her mother thought she was involved in some "foolish escapade with some other young girl," but she mounted a search after "not hearing from her for two or three days." Mrs. Adair and her other daughter found Dora in Denver with the help of T. Jeff Carr, a former United States marshal.

Virginia found Dora at the Union Hotel and told her that her brother Gilbert had died four months earlier, and he had "died calling to her." Dora "promised" to return home but said she first needed to "run over to my room first and tell my roommate" because it would be "cruel not to let her know."

Dora fled, leaving her hotel room unlocked and bare. Neighbors said she was known to them as "Belle," and her mother had died. "Mr. Morris," her husband, was out of work, so she pawned her goods and chattels to drive the wolf from the door. She told others she fled to Denver to get away from her "perfect tyrant" of a mother.

Neighbors described "Frank Morris" as "about 30 years old" and slightly bald on top, with hair tipped somewhat with gray, and he had a heavy mustache.

Dora's mystery man was Captain Frank A. Hubble, a forty-eight-year-old divorcé with a daughter Dora's age. He was known in Grand Army circles for his tales of how he escaped from a Confederate prisoner-of-war camp at Andersonville, Georgia. Denver-area police knew Hubble as a confidence man who was hired to sell lightning rods in Boulder but instead fled with a $125 advance.

The only one who had known of Dora's whereabouts was Mrs. Brown, a dressmaker Dora worked for in Cheyenne. A package of letters written by Mrs. Brown was found in Dora's vacant hotel room. The *Cheyenne Daily Leader* said:

> [The letters'] *purport was to the effect that the girl's mother was "the old d---l," and to be sure to avoid her, as she was coming to Denver to find her. Mrs. Brown also promised to come to Denver to "help keep the pursuers off the track"....The entire detective force of Denver is again trying to locate the couple. Whatever their motive for hiding and trying to elude Mrs. Adair may be there is no doubt but they are pretty shrewd and had given the "sleuths" of Denver a lively and fruitless chase.*

A headline in a Denver newspaper summed up the bizarre tale: "Turns Up Again. Dora Adair, the Runaway Girl from Cheyenne, Attracts Attention Again."

A reprinted article found in the *Cheyenne Daily Leader* said Dora gave birth prematurely at a house located at 1840 Champs Street. "Authorities will investigate the case to see if any crime exists."

Dora's father died in Fort Collins, Colorado, in October 1907. His obituary said Dora was married and lived in Central City, Colorado. Virginia Adair died on January 19, 1909. Her obituary in the *Weekly Courier* of Fort Collins said: "Mrs. Adair was a kind-hearted woman, a good neighbor and true friend and a devoted wife and mother. She leaves one married daughter whose home is in Denver." In a probate notice in the *Weekly Courier*, Virginia Adair willed "all of my property, personal, real or mixed, be given to my daughter, Dora Hazard, after the payment of all just debts and funeral expenses as well as expenses of administration."

Dora's final resting place is unknown.

Private Gertrude Douglas

Gertrude Douglas was born in Brooklyn, Iowa, on March 9, 1868. She is the daughter of Thomas and Eliza Douglas. Gertrude had one sister, Ida May, and a brother, Richard.

Thomas settled in Cheyenne in 1869 and found work as a Cheyenne police officer. Gertrude married John Martin Von Kennel, a postal worker, on December 29, 1892. The couple had two sons, Stanley and Merritt, and two daughters, Wynona and Frances.

Gertrude died on October 9, 1927, and was buried at Lakeview Cemetery.

Private Minnie Gape

Minnie Gape was born in Cleveland, Ohio, on September 16, 1876. She is the daughter of Joseph and Sarah Gape. Joseph was a member of the Durant Fire Department. Both parents were active in the Episcopal church and supported many charity events. She had three brothers, William, James and John, and a sister, Mary.

The spring of 1895 was a tragic one for the Gape family as scarlet fever claimed three family members in a matter of weeks. Mary—who was also known as Minnie, causing some confusion—died on March 25, 1895. The *Laramie Boomerang*, dated March 25, 1895, said:

> *Minnie Gape, the little girl who was reported dead on Friday evening from the effects of scarlet fever, passed away yesterday and was buried last night at midnight. To-day it was reported that a little sister was down with the disease, and two others near the residence at the corner of Twenty-fifth and O'Neill streets.*
>
> *There was a good deal of alarm expressed in the neighborhood of the Gape residence because some clothing belonging to the dead girl had been hung on a line in the yard. This clothing had been properly disinfected under the direction of a physician, so that there was no danger from it. The authorities are doing all in their power to see that all cases are properly quarantined, and in this they are being ably seconded by the people and the physicians. Three new cases were reported to the mayor to-day. She was thirteen years old.*[45]

Willie died at sixteen on March 29, and Johnnie died April 14, 1895, when he was six.

Minnie sang and participated in theater during her school years. She graduated from the University of Wyoming in the fall of 1893 and taught in Uva, Wyoming, in 1893 and in Cheyenne in 1895. She married Osgood Johnson on September 23, 1896. Osgood was a native of Baltimore,

Maryland, who moved to Cheyenne in the spring of 1882 to work for the National Cattle Company. He later worked for the Swan Land and Cattle Company before settling near Uva in 1886.

Osgood died in 1941. Minnie died on June 30, 1957, and is buried in the Wheatland cemetery.

Private Kittie Gordon

Kittie Gordon was born in New Jersey in 1871. She is recorded in the Wyoming territorial census of 1880 as a boarder in the household of John Freel and his sisters, Agnes and Jennie. John Freel was a prominent freight hauler for Camp Carlin.

Kittie participated in the Holmes Literary Society, supported Catholic charities and events, lobbied against gambling in Cheyenne and did laundry for the first state legislature. Kittie attended the company debut at Keefe Hall and is on the statehood parade roster, but she does not appear in the company photograph taken at the capitol steps.

Private Levina Grainger

Levina Grainger was born in Cheyenne, Wyoming Territory, on February 3, 1873. She was also known as Levinia Grainger and Levina Granger. She is the daughter of Joseph and Mary Grainger. Her parents immigrated to the United States and settled in Cheyenne in 1869. Territorial census records from 1880 said Levina had five brothers, Joseph, Charles, Franklin, Albert and John.

The elder Joseph was a member of the First Territorial Council, a city councilman for three years, a mechanic for the Union Pacific and a Baptist minister. Mary was active in the Baptist church, a member of the Woman's Christian Temperance Union and a state superintendent for Work among Railroad Workers.

Levina was an accomplished pianist, a member of the Holmes Literary Society and a bicycle enthusiast. She attended public schools but is not listed among the graduates.

She married Frank Radcliffe in Cheyenne in 1902 and moved to Sumner, Nebraska, where Frank owned a contracting business. The couple had three daughters, Mary Ann, Lily and Levina; and four sons, Reginald, William,

Levina Grainger, *left*, was appointed an engrossing clerk for the Wyoming state legislature in 1897.

Charles and Albert. Levina moved to California with her daughter Mary after Frank died but returned to the region and settled in Eagle, Colorado, in 1947. She later purchased the Eagle Valley Telephone Company and Morgan Manor hotel.

Levina died on July 17, 1952. She was buried at the Eagle Cemetery. She was survived by three daughters, four sons and ten grandchildren. Her obituary said she was preceded in death by her husband, eight brothers and two sisters who died in infancy en route to America from England.

Private Gretchen Hermann

Gretchen Hermann is the daughter of F.C. Hermann. F.C. was an irrigation and drainage investigator for the Department of Agriculture. He worked in Wyoming, Arizona, New Mexico and Colorado. There was also a Cheyenne business called Hermann's that advertised evening shades, moire silks and beaded fringe. Gretchen was a member of the Holmes Literary Society, but little else is known of her.

Private Mamie Layden

Mamie Layden is the daughter of James Layden, a carpenter for the Union Pacific Railroad. The earliest record of the Layden family in Cheyenne is September 3, 1884, when James filed a deed for lot six, block 101, for fifty dollars. The family resided at 420 East Fifteenth Street until they moved to Denver in 1892. Mamie married Theodore Boer, a member of the U.S. Army, in Arapaho, Colorado, on January 1, 1893. Mamie died the following year and is buried in Cheyenne. The *Cheyenne Daily Leader* dated May 25, 1894, said:

> *The remains of Mrs. Theo. Boer, formerly Miss Mamie Layden, of this city will arrive on the Denver train at 1:40 p.m., Sunday. Friends of the family and the I.O.O.F., are invited to meet and escort the remains to the cemetery.*
>
> *The Rev. J.M. Brown of the south side Congregational church will officiate.*

Mamie is buried in the Odd Fellow Cemetery under the name Mamie Layden.

Private Frances Moore

Frances Moore was born in Cheyenne in 1874. She is the daughter of Horace and Abbie Moore. Frances had three older sisters, Eva, Charlotte and Maggie, and two brothers, Horace and Jared. The senior Horace was a pharmacist and hospital steward during the Civil War. He settled in Cheyenne in 1872; worked as an Indian agent, foreman for the *Cheyenne Leader* and coroner; and was an honorary member of the Alert Hose Company.

Frances was an original member of Company H, but she did not march in the Wyoming statehood parade. She married Charles Elmer Martin on December 15, 1892. The *Cheyenne Daily Sun* said:

> *Francis Isabella, youngest daughter of Mr. and Mrs. H.W. Moore, and Chas. E. Martin, a Cheyenne young man of sterling worth, were united in marriage last evening at the home of the bride's parents on East Nineteenth. Quite a number of friends of the family witnessed the performance of the ceremony by Rev. Geo. C. Ricker. Miss Margaret Moore was bridesmaid*

and Mr. Albert Trump best man. An elaborate wedding supper was served.
The presents were numerous and valuable. Mr. and Mrs. Martin are
already at home at 817 East Sixteenth. The bride has spent her life in
Cheyenne and is highly esteemed by all.

Private May Oakley

Sarah May Oakley was born in May 1876 in Indiana. She is the daughter of William and Julia Oakley. She had a brother, Thomas.

William Oakley was a member of the Cheyenne Fire Department and fraternal organizations. He died on September 11, 1888. The *Cheyenne Sun* said, "Mr. Oakley has resided in Cheyenne for many years and was one of the best known and most respected citizens of the city and his loss will be deeply deplored by all." Julia was active in the church community.

May married Leo Leffler in a private ceremony at the family home located at 212 East Ninth Street on June 29, 1904. The wedding was a quiet affair attended by about twenty relatives and intimate friends. The *Wyoming Tribune* dated June 29, 1904, said, "The groom is a well-known young shop man employed by the Union Pacific, while the bride is a charming and accomplished young lady who has resided in the city since her childhood."

The couple had one daughter, Julia Ann, born in 1905, who died of heart problems on September 10, 1915. May donated her copy of the official statehood photograph of Company H taken at the capitol to the Wyoming State Archives in 1940. The photograph has numbers above each of the nineteen members present, and the names of all members were recorded for posterity. A side feature with the photograph May donated was published in the *Annals of Wyoming* in April 1965.

May died in Cheyenne in 1952 and is buried in Lakeview Cemetery.

Private Maud Post

Maud Post was born in Cheyenne in 1875. She is the daughter of Fredrick and Catherine Post. Fredrick was an engineer for the Union Pacific Railroad, operating between Cheyenne and Sidney, Nebraska. He also served several terms on the city council. Maud had two brothers, Martin and Freddie, the latter of whom died on January 10, 1883, shortly after his first birthday. The family resided at Seventeenth and Bent.

Newspapers described her as "beautiful and accomplished." She married James Sweeney, a pack train leader, at Cheyenne Depot on April 21, 1896. The couple eventually moved to Kansas, where James later hauled freight at Fort Robinson.

Maud died in 1947 and is buried in Mount Olivet Cemetery in Cheyenne.

Private Marcelline Rouleau

Marcelline Rouleau was born in Cheyenne in 1873. She is the daughter of Robert "Albert" and Wilhemina Rouleau. She had two brothers, Charles and Francis, and one sister, Adeline.

Albert was a real estate speculator whose last name was spelled *Roulon* in the Wyoming Territorial Census of 1880 and as *Rouleon* on the marriage license issued by the City of Cheyenne on March 30, 1873. Marcelline's name was spelled *Marsle* in the 1880 census and *Morcelline* in her obituary. The family moved to Silver Bow, Montana, around April 1891. Marcelline died on November 22, 1898, and was buried at Mount Moriah Cemetery in Butte, Montana.

The *Cheyenne Daily Sun-Leader*, dated November 22, 1898, reprinted a telegram sent to Mrs. John St. John's of Cheyenne regarding the death of her niece. The article said:

> *Morcelline Rouleau Dead. Morcelline Rouleau, who is a niece of Mrs. John Saint John of this city, will be remembered by our young people as having attended our high school a few years ago. The Rouleau family resided in Cheyenne for some years. Miss Rouleau belonged to the Methodist church in this city and was a charming, young lady, esteemed by all who knew her. The news of her death will be a shock to her many friends.*

Private Mamie Thompson

Mary "Mamie" Thompson was born in Wisconsin in 1874. She is the daughter of James E. and Ella Thompson. Mamie had a sister, Nelly. Indications are that James and his extended family ranched in Sweetwater, Carbon, Platte and Laramie Counties. Mamie participated in school recitals and graduated from high school in 1892.

Mamie Thompson, *second row, third from left*, and the high school class of 1892.

An inscription on the back of an old Central School photograph says that Mamie married Tom O'Neil. Records show the city clerk issued a marriage license to a Thomas D. O'Neil on April 29, 1895, but Cheyenne newspapers did not record the union.

Private Mattie Thompson

Maude "Mattie" Thompson was born in Cheyenne in 1873. She is the daughter of George and Catherine Thompson. Mattie had two brothers, Charles and George. The senior George hauled freight, and Catherine operated a small candy store on Seventeenth Street between Ferguson and Eddy.

Maude married Charles Jamison on September 7, 1892. The *Daily Sun* said:

> *One of the most brilliant weddings of the year occurred last evening at the residence of Mr. and Mrs. George E. Thompson, on Capitol avenue,*

between Nineteenth and Twentieth. The bride was the beautiful and accomplished daughter of the house, Miss Maude Thompson, and the groom was Charles A. Jamison, a sturdy, bright and popular employee at the Union Pacific shops. Rev. A.G. Lane, pastor of the First Presbyterian church, performed the ceremony in the presence of a large company of friends of the family.

The marriage was solemnized at 8 o'clock. The wedding procession was from the large parlor on the second floor of the house. It was led by little Clara Robinson, daughter of F.L. Robinson. She was in an elaborate costume of white and rose colored-silk and white silk lace, with trimmings of roses, a large corsage bouquet and a large basket of roses. The bride was in a rich-ashes of roses gown, en train, trimmed with corded silk, corsage bouquet. Miss Annie May Stanley was bridesmaid. She wore a costume of gray silk, with heavy corsage bouquet.

…Mr. and Mrs. Jamison will forego a tour. They are already established in a neat little home on East Sixteenth street.[46]

Private Minnie Thompson

Minnie Thompson was born in Missouri in 1877. She is the daughter of John and Sarah Thompson. Minnie had two brothers, Lecasta and Edward. John Thompson was a surveyor general for Laramie County in 1886 and chairman of the Democratic Party in 1893.

Very little is known of Minnie Thompson other than the fact that the Laramie county clerk issued a marriage license on October 8, 1896, to Henry R. Sayres and Miss Minnie Thompson.

Private Jennie Tupper

Private Jennie Tupper was born in Iowa on March 9, 1873. She is the daughter of Wilbur and Margaret Tupper. Jennie had two younger brothers, Harry and Wiley, and two younger sisters, Mabel and Jessie. Wilbur was the owner of Model Market, located at 215 West Seventeenth Street.

Jennie was active in her church and was described as intelligent, quiet and a talented speaker and musician. She graduated in June 1891. The *Wyoming Commonwealth* dated June 14, 1891, said:

Miss Jennie Tupper has grown up almost a stranger to many of us until we made her acquaintance in the literary exercises of the class, and as from time to time she appeared before us on the rostrum we were struck by her fine appearance and pleasant delivery. She is the daughter of one of our genial business men, and her father being a musician Miss Jennie also inherits much musical ability.

The newspaper added: "She is one of the brightest in her studies, and her teachers predict a busy, useful life in her occupation as a teacher." Jennie worked as a private secretary for John Wesley Lacey, the attorney who defended the infamous outlaw Tom Horn in 1903. She was so disturbed by the guilty verdict that she would not discuss the trial, even in close family circles. Chip Carlson said in his book *Tom Horn: Killing Men Is My Specialty* that Jennie Tupper eventually shared her feelings about the Tom Horn case during a KOA radio broadcast on local history in the 1930s.

Her obituary, from the *Wyoming Tribune*, dated June 2, 1966, said:

Services are pending for Miss Jennie M. Tupper, 93, of 2121 Van Lennen Ave., a pioneer Wyoming resident, who died Wednesday at home.

She had been a resident of Cheyenne since 1886. She had been a secretary. Miss Tupper began her secretarial career with Judge Lacey and continued with firm of Loomis and Lazear where she worked for 52 years. She retired from her position with the firm at age of 80.

Jennie's obituary continued:

Miss Tupper had been a member of Company H of the Girl Guards who participated in Wyoming Day ceremonies when Wyoming became a state.

She was a member of the Congregational church for 70 years and was also a member of Mizpah chapter 36 of the Order of Eastern Star, and the King's Daughters.

Survivors include a sister, Mrs. Orren C. Babbitt of Cheyenne; and several nieces and nephews. She was preceded in death by a sister, Mrs. Mabel Yeager and a brother, Harry W. Tupper.

Jennie Tupper died on June 1, 1966 and was buried in the Lakeview Cemetery.

The kepi that Jennie wore and the rifle she carried in the Wyoming statehood parade were donated to the Wyoming State Museum in 1970 by the family of Jessie Tupper Babbitt.

Private Mabel Tupper

Mabel Tupper was born on November 1, 1874. She is the daughter of Wilbur and Margaret Tupper. Mabel had two brothers, Harry and Wiley, and two sisters, Jennie and Jessie. She graduated with the class of 1893. Very little is known of Mabel other than that she won awards as a seamstress. Mabel married Walter Yeager, a mail carrier and artist, in a private ceremony in Cheyenne on June 12, 1893. The couple had one daughter, Eula. They lived at 2103 Evans Avenue.

Mabel died on September 19, 1960, and was buried in Lakeview Cemetery in Cheyenne.

Her family donated the rifle and kepi she carried in the statehood parade and a white silk ribbon with hand-painted gold lettering that Mabel wore to the Wyoming State Museum in 1970.

Private Bertha Wedemeyer

Bertha Wedemeyer was born in Wyoming on October 25, 1875. She is the daughter of John and Dora Wildermyer (spelling later changed). Bertha had three brothers, Theo, John and Frank, and one sister, Mary. John was a member of the Wyoming state senate and served on the Agriculture Committee.

Bertha graduated from high school in June 1893. She taught in Los Angeles, California, and Las Animas, Colorado. She married Ernest Boomer, a commissary sergeant, on August 15, 1906. The couple had one son, Bruce. Ernest died on June 27, 1919, and is buried at Sunnyside Cemetery in Long Beach, California. Bertha died on October 23, 1971, and is buried next to Ernest.

Private Marie Wedemeyer

Mary "Marie" Wedemeyer was born in Keil, Germany, on July 25, 1872. She is the daughter of John and Dora Wildermyer (spelling later changed). She had three brothers, Theo, John and Frank, and one sister, Bertha. The *Wyoming Commonwealth* dated June 14, 1891, predicted Marie would be a teacher:

Miss Marie H. Wedemeyer took the honors of the class as valedictorian. She is a young lady whose home is on the south side, and is, I believe, the first graduate from the newer part of the city. Her quick, bright manner makes her a genuine favorite with all pupils and teachers. She is one of the strongest scholars in the class and is devoted to her studies. She is expected to follow the profession of teaching and has a fine position already in view. She has numerous relatives among us and her bright scholarly career is the source of much pride to them, and many over the salt sea in the dear old fatherland.[47]

Marie entered the teaching profession, working as a substitute in Cheyenne in September 1891, before teaching third grade full time in May 1893 at Johnson School. Boulder College (Colorado) offered her a faculty position teaching German in 1901, but she declined the offer and enrolled at Columbia College in New York. Marie taught in Brooklyn until her death on October 14, 1924. Her remains were interred in the Odd Fellow Cemetery in Cheyenne under the name Marie Wedemeyer.

Chapter 8

Stitzer's Other Guards

C ompany K was Colonel Frank Stitzer's best-known drill team, but he did have other successful drill teams. Company B held its first dress drill and ball at the armory located in Keefe Hall on Friday, May 24, 1889. The newspapers described the team as made up of "four awkward men." Company B developed into a reputable drill team and was invited to New York for the centennial celebration of President George Washington's inauguration in 1889.

The men of Company B attended a Fourth of July parade in Denver, Colorado, presided over by General Tecumseh Sherman in 1889 and served as guards of honor at a Grand Army of the Republic event on December 30, 1889. They marched in a Decoration Day parade in Cheyenne in 1890 and the Wyoming statehood parade held on July 23, 1890.

Stitzer also trained a group of twenty-one boys and girls from Cheyenne's society known as Stitzer's Guards about a year before the Company K debut. The team performed at the Presbyterian fundraiser held on August 25, 1898, at Keefe Hall.

The *Cheyenne Daily Leader* listed Archie Hale, Charles Bonfils, George Gregory, Harry Griffith, Emma O'Brien, Gertrude Morgan, Lester Baker, Fred Chaffin, Jessie Moonlight, Clara Neuman, Laura Larsh, Mamie Horrie, Emma Schilling, Gertrude Dobbins, Edith Rowen, Mina McGregor, Bessie Vreeland, Grace Chaffin, Belle Smalley, Emma Griffith and George Artist as members of the drill team.

George Artist is the son of Andrew and Louisa Artist. Andrew worked for the Union Pacific Railroad.

Lester Baker is the son of Lester Baker. The senior Baker served as F.E. Warren's secretary during his political career in Wyoming and Washington, D.C.

Charles Bonfils is the son of Eugene Napolean and Henrietta Bacon Lewis Bonfils. Eugene Napolean was a federal agent for the territory land office and later served as a judge. Henrietta is a member of the distinguished Meriwether Lewis family and is related to President George Washington (her father's cousin married George Washington's sister).

Fred Chaffin is the son of John and Mary Chaffin. His sister Grace was an original member of Company K. John worked as county clerk and ex-officio register of deeds. He left government work sometime during the early 1880s to start a successful floral business.

Gertrude Dobbins is the daughter of Asa and Emma Dobbins. Asa was a military meteorologist and the first weatherman in Cheyenne. Emma was a friend of Colonel Jay Torrey of Torrey Rough Rider fame.

George Gregory is the son of Eugene George Gregory. Eugene was a lieutenant colonel on the Wyoming National Guard regimental staff. George Gregory became a county assessor and was picked to serve on the coroner's jury investigating the death of Willie Nickell, the fourteen-year-old boy allegedly shot by Tom Horn.

Emma and Harry Griffith are the children of Harry and Emma Griffith. The Griffiths are said to be descendants of the Griffith family that emigrated from England with William Penn, the founder of Pennsylvania.

Archie Hale is the son of William and Josie Hale. William was appointed the fourth governor of the Wyoming Territory on July 18, 1882, by President Chester Arthur. Governor William Hale served from August 3, 1882, until his death on January 13, 1885.

Laura Larsh is the daughter of Charles and Emma Larsh. Her parents appear in a Collated Claims Report of the Senate Committee dated 1898 as receiving $1,632.98 from the Cheyenne Land Office. Laura's name appeared frequently in the Cheyenne social column until January 12, 1901, when the *Cheyenne Daily Leader* said she moved to Denver to teach.

Jessie Moonlight is the daughter of Thomas Moonlight. Thomas was a Civil War veteran and former governor of the Wyoming Territory from 1887 to 1889.

Edith Rowen is the daughter of James Rowen, an attorney.

Emma O'Brien, Gertrude Morgan, Clara Newman, Mamie Horrie, Mina McGregor, Bessie Vreeland, Grace Chaffin and Belle Smalley continued their careers as members of Company K. Emma Schilling joined Company H.

Colonel Stitzer trained another group of girls just before the turn of the century. The group performed a style of drill originated by a group known as the Zoauves. The Zouaves were a light infantry corps in the French army who served in North Africa in 1830. They drilled with rifles with large bayonets and wore a colorful oriental-style uniform. Zoauve-style drills gained popularity after the Civil War, especially among state militias.

Stitzer's performed during a three-day Grand Army of the Republic event held at Keefe Hall. There were twenty members who performed—sixteen regular performers and four reserve members. The *Daily Sun-Leader* dated January 20, 1898, said:

> *It is expected the place will be filled tonight, as the concert by the Eighth infantry band, one of the best organizations of the kind in the west, will be given, and the reserved maneuvers of the twenty beautiful girls will be given, Col. Stitzer conducting the drill. Those who witnessed the zouave drill last night will be sure to see the additional evolutions of Col. Stitzer.*

Chapter 9

Girl Cadets of Rawlins

The Girl Cadets, from the western Wyoming town of Rawlins, were inspired by Company K. The group organized about two weeks before Company H and was trained by the Reverend Bewley, who used the *Reed Infantry Tactics* manual as a training guide. The *Rawlins Republican* said, "Rev. Bewley has procured gun[s] for the use of the girl cadets. It might probably be well to state that the guns are harmless, in case any of the fair members of the company should desire to use them with malicious or felonious intent."[48]

Their first public appearance was on April 23, 1890, at a Methodist church fundraiser held at the opera house in Rawlins. An article in the *Rawlins Republican* dated April 25, 1890, said:

> *An event of the past week which gives the* Republican *much pleasure to record is the entertainment given by the Girl Cadets of Rawlins. Preparations for this entertainment were in progress some five or six weeks before it was given to the public. It was generally known all this while, however, that the young ladies were preparing something out of the usual rotine [routine] of church socials or entertainment. The exercise was given at the opera house on Tuesday evening and notwithstanding that rain continued to fall in torrents until 8 o'clock, when the curtain arose at 8:30 a large house had assembled to greet the handsome performers.*
>
> *The young ladies were dressed very becoming and presented a natty and attractive appearance. They each wore a navy blue, fireman's cap and blue muslin dresses, tastefully trimmed with white cord and a row of white pearl*

buttons down the front. They were provided with mock bayonets, and went through the manual of arms in a manner that would do credit to any old veteran. They were loudly cheered and, peradventure, felt themselves well repaid for the many weeks of toil spent in preparation.

The proceeds of the entertainment netted a sum which was very satisfactory to all concerned. It is earnestly hoped that this fair company will remain under training so they can appear in case of a statehood celebration.[49]

The Rawlins Girl Cadets' final public appearance was at the Decoration Day ceremonies held in Rawlins. The *Rawlins Republican* said:

The weather was clear, cool and calm. The city donned a regular holiday appearance and the stars and stripes floated from nearly every business building. Early in the morning members of the three different fire companies in uniform were strolling hither and thither through the city. Later on, the girl cadets dressed in their natty blue uniforms made their appearance on the streets, all adding to the general appearance of the holiday atire [attire].[50]

Decoration Day began with a band procession to the cemetery followed by the Girl Cadets, the Casper W. Collins Post, Vigilance Hose Company No. One, the Hook and Ladder Company and "citizens in carriages, on horseback and foot." The Grand Army of the Republic held a solemn service at the graves of the dead comrades, and a small detachment from the Girl Cadets "covered the graves over with beautiful wreaths of flowers."

There are no records of the Rawlins Girl Cadets after the Decoration Day parade.

Chapter 10

Girl Cadets of Laramie

Rumors of a new company of Girl Guards in Laramie appeared in the July 24, 1890 edition of the *Boomerang* under a local gossip column on page four. The brief article said, "There is talk of organizing a company of Girl Guards in Laramie."

The new company did not debut until after the turn of the century. The *Laramie Republic* announced the formation of the new company in its December 5, 1902 edition under the headline "Girls."

A *Laramie Republic* article said the Girls' Cadet Corps would participate in Governor Deforest Richards's inauguration in Cheyenne on January 5, 1903, provided "the girls" were uniformed and properly drilled by that time. An article in the *Laramie Republican* dated January 9, 1903, suggests that uniforms did not arrive before the inauguration: "The young ladies and young gentlemen belonging to the cadet corps at the university had their first drill together this afternoon, appearing as four companies on the campus in front of the university. Most of the girls wore their blue and white uniforms. It was an inspirational sight."[51]

The Girls' Cadet Corps drilled with wooden rifles modeled after the Winchester rifle at least four and a half hours weekly. In January 1903, two companies of Girls' Cadets, numbering 27 members, performed an exhibition drill for the state legislature and 150 Cheyenne citizens who toured the university.

The *Laramie Republican* said:

The *Laramie Republic* newspaper used sex appeal to announce the organization of the Laramie Girl Cadets.

The garrison flag was waving in the wind from the top of the flagstaff, and on the campus in front of the university were drawn up the four companies of the cadet corps, commanded by Captain Yates and the officers of the different companies. Particularly noticeable and heartily applauded were the two companies of young ladies, Companies C and D. The uniforms of the girls are very striking and the officers of the companies have brought the young ladies to a remarkable degree of proficiency in both the drill and manual [of arms].[52]

A bizarre article was printed in the *Cheyenne Daily Leader* in 1903 during a slow news day. A summary regarding the Girl Cadets said William H. Holliday of Laramie proposed a bill to reorganize the Wyoming National Guard under the supervision and command of the Salvation Army corps of Cheyenne. This bill provided that the ranking company of the regiment would be the Girl Cadets of Laramie.[53]

The Girls' Cadet Corps disbanded at the start of the United States' involvement in World War I. A blue and white dress worn by the Girl Cadets and a wooden rifle issued to cadets is displayed at the Laramie Plains Museum.

Notes

Introduction

1. Carroll, "Girl Guards."

Chapter 1

2. *Cheyenne Daily Leader*, "General."
3. *Wyoming Commonwealth*, "Girl Guards of Wyoming."
4. *Cheyenne Daily Leader*, "Attention Everybody."

Chapter 2

5. *Cheyenne Weekly Sun*, "High School Cadets."
6. Walker, "Wyoming Plan of Military Training."
7. *Cheyenne Sun*, "Rousing Reception."
8. *Cheyenne Daily Leader*, "Female Militia."
9. *Cheyenne Weekly Sun*, "Sun Spots."
10. *Cheyenne Daily Sun*, "Second Night."
11. *Daily Sun*, "Company K Drill."
12. *Daily Sun*, "Girl Guards, Company K."

Chapter 3

13. *Cheyenne Daily Sun*, "Rousing Reception."
14. *Cheyenne Weekly Sun*, "Girl Guards."
15. *Cheyenne Sun*, "Girl Guards."
16. *Cheyenne Sun*, "Our Dead Heroes."
17. *Cheyenne Daily Sun Illustrated*, "A Great Day."
18. *Wyoming Commonwealth*, "Commencement Day."
19. *Cheyenne Daily Leader*, "Drill and Hop."

Chapter 5

20. *Cheyenne Weekly Sun*, "Gossip About the Guards."
21. *Cheyenne Daily Leader*, "Carnival."

Chapter 6

22. *Cheyenne Daily Leader*, "Carnival."
23. *Cheyenne Weekly Sun*, "Girl Guard Benefit."
24. Works Progress Administration, "Argesheimer Family."
25. *Cheyenne Daily Sun*, "Military Girls."
26. *Cheyenne Daily Sun*, "Company H, Girl Guards."
27. *Cheyenne Daily Sun*, "Ready for War."

Chapter 7

28. *Cheyenne Daily Leader*, "Miss O'Brien Dead."
29. *Cheyenne Leader*, "Cheyenne Lady Married."
30. *Cheyenne Daily Leader*, "Their Wedding Day."
31. *Daily Boomerang*, "Cheyenne Wedding."
32. *Cheyenne Sun*, "Matrimonials."
33. *Cheyenne Daily Sun*, "Marriage of Gertrude Ellis."
34. *Cheyenne Daily Leader*, "Married."
35. *Cheyenne Daily Leader*, "Pneumonia Kills Pioneer Freighter."
36. *Wyoming Tribune*, "General Pershing's Son a Fine Boy."
37. *Wyoming Tribune*, "Goldstein-Ringolsky."

38. *Cheyenne Daily Sun*, "Brilliant Wedding."
39. *Cheyenne Daily*, "Wedding."
40. *Cheyenne Daily Leader*, "Granted a Divorce."
41. *Cheyenne Daily Leader*, "Charged with Bigamy."
42. *Cheyenne Daily Leader*, "Social Life in Cheyenne."
43. Works Progress Administration, "Argesheimer Family."
44. *Cheyenne Daily Sun*, "Happily Married."
45. *Boomerang*, "Scarlet Fever."
46. *Daily Sun*, "Was a Pretty Wedding."
47. *Wyoming Commonwealth*, "Commencement Day."

Chapter 9

48. *Rawlins Republican*, "Around About Town."
49. *Rawlins Republican*, "Girl Cadets."
50. *Rawlins Republican*, "Decoration Day in Rawlins

Chapter 10

51. *Laramie Republican*, "Girls and Boys Drill Together."
52. *Laramie Republican*, "Legislature Visits University."
53. *Laramie Republican*, "Third House."

Bibliography

A.W. Bowen and Company. *Progressive Men of Wyoming.* "General Frank A. Stitzer," 30–31. N.p., 1905.

Carroll, Wesley Philemon. "The Girl Guards." *Cheyenne Weekly Sun*, February 20, 1890.

Cheyenne Daily Leader. "Attention Everybody." June 21, 1883, 3.

———. "The Carnival." October 23, 1889, 3.

———. "Charged with Bigamy." October 9, 1894, 3.

———. "Drill and Hop." September 5, 1890, 3.

———. "Female Militia." October 22, 1889, 1.

———. "Found and Lost Her." February 28, 1891, 3.

———. "General." September 24, 1869, 1.

———. "Granted a Divorce." October 9, 1894, 3.

———. "Married." September 5, 1894, 3.

———. "Miss O'Brien Dead." December 12, 1900, 4.

———. "Pneumonia Kills Pioneer Freighter." May 8, 1908, 8.

———. "Social Life in Cheyenne." October 7, 1904, 5.

———. "Their Wedding Day." May 24, 1894, 1.

Cheyenne Daily Sun. "A Brilliant Wedding." April 26, 1892, 3.

———. "Company H, Girl Guards." May 16, 1890, 5.

———. "Happily Married." October 20, 1892, 3.

———. "Marriage of Gertrude Ellis." November 18, 1892, 3.

———. "The Military Girls." April 17, 1890, 5.

———. "Ready for War." July 15, 1890, 5.

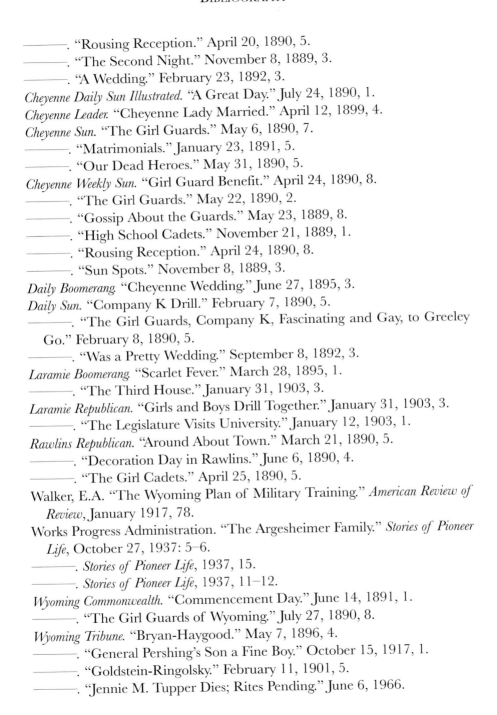

———. "Rousing Reception." April 20, 1890, 5.

———. "The Second Night." November 8, 1889, 3.

———. "A Wedding." February 23, 1892, 3.

Cheyenne Daily Sun Illustrated. "A Great Day." July 24, 1890, 1.

Cheyenne Leader. "Cheyenne Lady Married." April 12, 1899, 4.

Cheyenne Sun. "The Girl Guards." May 6, 1890, 7.

———. "Matrimonials." January 23, 1891, 5.

———. "Our Dead Heroes." May 31, 1890, 5.

Cheyenne Weekly Sun. "Girl Guard Benefit." April 24, 1890, 8.

———. "The Girl Guards." May 22, 1890, 2.

———. "Gossip About the Guards." May 23, 1889, 8.

———. "High School Cadets." November 21, 1889, 1.

———. "Rousing Reception." April 24, 1890, 8.

———. "Sun Spots." November 8, 1889, 3.

Daily Boomerang. "Cheyenne Wedding." June 27, 1895, 3.

Daily Sun. "Company K Drill." February 7, 1890, 5.

———. "The Girl Guards, Company K, Fascinating and Gay, to Greeley Go." February 8, 1890, 5.

———. "Was a Pretty Wedding." September 8, 1892, 3.

Laramie Boomerang. "Scarlet Fever." March 28, 1895, 1.

———. "The Third House." January 31, 1903, 3.

Laramie Republican. "Girls and Boys Drill Together." January 31, 1903, 3.

———. "The Legislature Visits University." January 12, 1903, 1.

Rawlins Republican. "Around About Town." March 21, 1890, 5.

———. "Decoration Day in Rawlins." June 6, 1890, 4.

———. "The Girl Cadets." April 25, 1890, 5.

Walker, E.A. "The Wyoming Plan of Military Training." *American Review of Review,* January 1917, 78.

Works Progress Administration. "The Argesheimer Family." *Stories of Pioneer Life,* October 27, 1937: 5–6.

———. *Stories of Pioneer Life,* 1937, 15.

———. *Stories of Pioneer Life,* 1937, 11–12.

Wyoming Commonwealth. "Commencement Day." June 14, 1891, 1.

———. "The Girl Guards of Wyoming." July 27, 1890, 8.

Wyoming Tribune. "Bryan-Haygood." May 7, 1896, 4.

———. "General Pershing's Son a Fine Boy." October 15, 1917, 1.

———. "Goldstein-Ringolsky." February 11, 1901, 5.

———. "Jennie M. Tupper Dies; Rites Pending." June 6, 1966.

Index

About the Author

Dan J. Lyon is a local historian and journalist who won top awards in National Collegiate Press Association competition and shares in two Air Force Space Command Museum of the Year Awards. He developed an interest in Wyoming's forgotten Girl Guard Militia while serving a five-year tour at F.E. Warren Air Force Base, the Air Force's oldest continuing military installation. Dan J. volunteers at the Warren ICBM and Heritage Museum, Wyoming National Guard Museum, at Fort D.A. Russell Open House, in classrooms and at his church. He is a member of the Warren Military Historic Association, the Laramie County Chapter of the Wyoming State Historical Society and the Cheyenne Genealogical and Historical Society.

Visit us at
www.historypress.com